FOLKTALE

and

HERO-TALE MOTIFS

in the

ODES OF PINDAR

FOLKTALE

and

HERO-TALE MOTIFS

in the

ODES OF PINDAR

by

MARY A. GRANT

UNIVERSITY OF KANSAS PRESS
LAWRENCE, 1967

Contents

61189

Introduction

"Sow from the hand, not from the whole sack!" was the rather tart advice concerning the use of mythological material given to young Pindar by the poetess Corinna. And to a youthful poet, eager to win commissions for victory odes from powerful patrons, the wealth of heroic tales that clung to the cities of Greece must have seemed tempting enough. There were natural limitations, it is true, to its free use, for these odes were to celebrate athletes of noble families, so that heroes of famous lineage, renowned for physical prowess rather than for intellectual attainments, would be chiefly appropriate. Though subjects probably were not dictated to the poet, tales of the victor's ancestors or home town would be taken for granted, or, if these failed, myths connected with the sites where the victories were won—Olympia, Delphi, Nemea, the Isthmus—might be used.

Many of Pindar's Epinician Odes (forty-five have been preserved) fulfill these conditions admirably. For the three in honor of victors from Cyrene he chose not only the myth of the nymph Cyrene, but also tales of Battus, one of the victor Arcesilas' ancestors; for Xenophon of Corinth, the tale of the city's most famous hero, Bellerophon; for victors from Aegina, the various exploits of the island's illustrious family, the Aeacidae; for Diagoras of Rhodes, the myth of the mysterious rise of the island from the sea, and the Sun God's claiming it for his own. Perhaps it would not be too rash to see the young poet feeling his way in the tenth *Pythian,* the earliest of the Odes, struggling between his attraction for the marvelous and the remote and his realization of the need for appropriateness, since, after dwelling on the tale of

1

Perseus among the Hyperboreans, a tale which had no real connection with the athlete celebrated, he rather self-consciously adds several lines of transition, almost as an apology for having digressed from his proper theme.

It would be natural, surely, for tales of Pindar's home city, Thebes, and for Aegina, so closely associated with it, to appear frequently. The problems for the many victors from Sicily, where there was scant mythological material to draw from, were difficult, and many disputes have arisen among critics as to the significance or appropriateness of the myths introduced in these fifteen odes. Is Pindar warning Hiero against the dangers of pride and extravagance in *Pythian* I and *Olympian* I in introducing such figures as Typhon and Tantalus? Finley has called Pindar the "symbolist beyond compare" among Greek poets, and speaks of the "heavy weight of meaning which Pindar's mythic figures carry," whereas Bacchylides' narrative, he thinks, is "simply narrative, and carries no such symbolic burden."[1] More concretely he suggests that the actual wars and political struggles of Pindar's own day may be prefigured in the tales. So he sees in Bellerophon's violence in *Isthmian* VII "the Athenians' will to rule," and in the portrayal of Odysseus in *Nemean* VIII "their insensibility to old standards." Bowra's chapter entitled "Echoes of Politics" in his *Pindar* gives other examples of this kind.[2]

Of all the heroes Heracles holds by far the most prominent place in the Odes, appearing in twenty-two of them. Not only was he a suitable figure in divine lineage and physical prowess but his myths were the most widely spread in the Greek world, and he could conveniently be introduced in connection with the

2

founding of the Olympic and Nemean Games as well if no other myth presented itself. Yet there is no doubt that he was also Pindar's ideal. "My heart is held by the theme of Heracles," he says in the first *Nemean*, and in *Pythian* IX he cries, "Foolish is the man whose tongue does not cleave to Heracles!"[3] Curious omissions are apparent, too, in the myths presented. Might Pindar's own (late) estrangement from Athens explain the absence of mythical references from the Theseus cycle? Why does he make no use of the rich material of the *Odyssey?* Such questions as to the poet's predilections may, however, conveniently be postponed until the material has been more fully analyzed.

The sources of the myths, as well as such questions of selection, have, of course, been discussed by critics in formal editions of the Odes. Comparisons with Homer and Hesiod have been made, as well as with Stesichorus and the poets of the Epic Cycle, so far as fragmentary material allows. But Pindar is a unique and baffling author, and many questions with regard to his sources remain unanswered. He seems to have been extraordinarily interested in local legends (naturally enough, considering the personal aspect of odes of victory)—legends which may never have been committed to writing, but which were relayed orally. Several phrases in the Odes indicate a use of tales told in both prose and verse by "former men," and in one particular instance—that dealing with the youth of Achilles—the reference seems to be especially to oral tales.[4]

Interest in and knowledge about oral narrative and folktales are comparatively recent, "receiving a great impetus," in the words of Stith Thompson, "in the last years of the nineteenth century." The rapid growth of such periodicals as the *Journal of American Folklore* (now in its seventy-ninth year) attests this activity, and in 1932-36 appeared the great Thompson *Motif-Index of Folk Literature* (revised, 1955-58), which catalogued and classified motifs from many sources both oral and written. "The ideal," as Thompson puts it in describing the planning of this *Motif-Index,* "was to bring together narrative elements from as many different fields of traditional fiction as possible."[5]

Andrew Lang was a pioneer among classicists in becoming conscious of this whole new approach to Greek and Latin material, and the large patterns of a few Greek and Roman folktales came to be recognized in such books as Halliday's *Greek and Roman Folklore* (1927) and Rose's *A Handbook of Greek Mythology* (1928), though of course literary material alone is available from the ancient world. But everything, both oral and literary, is grist to the folklorist's mill, and separate motifs from Greek mythology, derived chiefly from Fox's *Greek and Roman Mythology* and Frazer's notes to his edition of Apollodorus, were entered in the *Motif-Index,* though Thompson recognized that this collection was far from being complete.

So far as classicists themselves are concerned, interest has lagged a little. H. M. and N. K. Chadwick in their lengthy work *The Growth of Literature* speak rather critically of Greek scholarship in this respect, referring to its "exclusiveness" and its "unwillingness to take account of analogies in other (barbaric) literatures."[6] Classical scholars should in fairness admit this blind spot, though loyalty and pride in the high achievements of the Greeks account for it in great part. That Greek mythology is "advanced" as compared with much primitive material is, of course, readily apparent. Many years ago Gilbert Murray gave evidence to show how expurgation had "cleansed" the Homeric poems of many of the grosser aspects of primitive tales. Such practices as cannibalism and torture of prisoners, the hocus-pocus of purification, and belief in magic, witchcraft, and the uncanny powers of the dead do not appear in the poems.[7] But much primitive material does remain there and still remains embedded in later Greek literature. Thompson himself estimated that a thorough examination of separate Greek authors would at least double the number of motifs from such authors in his *Motif-Index*.[8]

The Chadwicks' criticism is generally true for Pindaric scholarship. The critical and school editions are mostly preoccupied with questions of text, literary source material, and interpretation, while actual analysis of mythical motifs and comparison of these with worldwide folklore motifs such as are catalogued in the Thompson *Motif-Index* remain untouched. An exception should be made, however, at once. Though references to folklore material in the index of Farnell's *Commentary* on Pindar are few, a careful reading of the notes reveals much material of this sort. Farnell's interest in Greek religious thought, evidenced by his authoritative works on hero cults and the like, led him to take a more than usual interest in what he might term the "lower theology of folklore." His references, however, do not often lead him to point out analogies with oral or written literatures.[9]

Though at first thought a comparison of motifs from the tales of a primitive society with the myths of so lofty an author as Pindar might seem absurd—the gap between them too great—some freshness of insight may be gained from the sharpness of the contrasts. The "Theban Eagle" can easily soar above such "indignities," and a measuring stick is a useful thing to have at hand in evaluation instead of vague references to "folklore material." Gilbert Murray, in the study mentioned above, differentiated the epic and the tragic "conventions" in the selection of mythical material;[10] perhaps some such conventions could be established for the lyric treatment in Epinician Odes. Pindar's own preferences at least can be indicated, and from the point of view of the folklorist, the accumulation of motifs may prove valuable for future studies. An appreciation of the vigor and imaginative power of some of the primitive tales will be an added benefit.

A survey of motifs in North American Indian oral tales, given in three chapters in Thompson's *The Folktale,* furnishes a convenient and compact source for such a comparison.[11] Since in such summaries the flavor of the original narrative is lost, primary material from which the motifs in the survey were derived—Thompson's *Tales of the North American Indians,* Coffin's *Indian Tales of North America,* Susan Feldman's *The Story-Telling Stone: Myths and Tales of the American Indians,* and other collections—has been used to supplement them.[12] In dealing with the material from Pindar one must remember that lyric treatment differs from ordinary narrative; it is brief and allusive. "The brightness of these songs of praise," the poet says, "flits beelike from theme to theme."[13] Of course the settings differ: a primitive society inhabiting a virgin wilderness and chiefly concerned with hunting and fishing will be contrasted with a developed culture where concerted war expeditions may move against walled cities, where kings rule a subject population, and man's venturings extend from the Straits of Gibraltar to the Nile and to the far north in a world at least semi-civilized. The constant presence of the gods and their close supervision of mortal affairs dominate the Odes. "What god, what hero, what man shall we praise?" the poet cries at the beginning of the second *Olympian*. An entirely different society is shown in the Indian tales. Women play a much more important part; many times old women are advisers or even formidable adversaries for the hero. The old grandmother, especially, takes care of the young hero, often equips him with magic objects, and watches his progress by means of a magic brew. These are the more obvious contrasts.

The material can be conveniently arranged first around generally recognized motifs of the hero tale as formulated by Thompson himself and by such critics as A. H. Krappe and Jan de Vries,[14] next by an assembling of motifs not directly connected with the hero tale. A classification of all the motifs after the manner of the Thompson *Index* follows.

Here, perhaps, the frequently made distinction between myth and folktale should be mentioned. The simplest differentiation is that myths are explanatory, while folktales have as their object sheer amusement. Thompson labels the first chapter of his *Motif-Index* "Mythological Motifs" and includes in it "motifs having to do with creation and with the nature of the world: creators, gods, and demigods; . . . the beginnings of life," and so forth. But difficulties of classification at once appear. The story of Hephaestus splitting open the head of Zeus for the birth of Athena might easily be classified as a myth of origin, but what of the tale of the same

Hephaestus devising a trick chair to which his mother sticks? This last is undoubtedly a folktale motif, found in the Grimm brothers' tale, "The Poor Man and the Rich Man," and elsewhere. Halliday himself admits that both myth and legend often borrow and employ elements which properly belong to folktale, though in themselves they differ from folktale because they have a purpose either explanatory or historical.[15] Scholars today seem to be insisting less and less on drawing such distinctions. So Franz Boas stated: "The facts that are brought out most clearly from a careful analysis of myths and folktales of an area like the northwest coast of America are that the contents of folktales and myths are largely the same, that the data show a continual flow from mythology to folktale and vice versa, and that neither group can claim priority."[16] Thompson, in the midst of the revision of his *Motif-Index of Folk-Literature* in 1955, in daily contact with thousands of narrative motifs from all parts of the world, concluded: "For most . . . of the body of folk narrative for primitive peoples everywhere, any differentiation between ordinary tale and myth is very minor."[17] J. R. R. Tolkien in his essay on the fairy tale in *Tree and Leaf* makes the same point. There is no fundamental distinction, he says, between the "higher and lower mythologies."[18]

Hero-Tale Motifs

The anthropologist John Greenway in a recent publication, *Literature among the Primitives,* has given a clear and comprehensive summary of modern methods of investigation in mythical research, differentiating and commenting on such groups of scholars as Linguistic Folklorists, Ritualists, Freudians, and the Historic-Geographic analysts of the Finnish school, as well as the anthropologists of his own field.[1] The first three have concerned themselves chiefly with questions of origin. For the systematization of mythical motifs and their organization into tale types the Finnish school—including Aarne, Krohn, and Thompson (who worked with Aarne and after his death revised his *Verzeichnis der Märchentypen*)—is chiefly responsible. In 1964 Archer Taylor, in an article entitled "The Biographical Pattern in Traditional Narrative," made a careful survey of the characteristics of a limited tale type, the Hero Tale, beginning with the simple Aryan Expulsion and Return formula of J. G. von Hahn (1871-76), and including such analyses as those of Otto Rank, Lord Raglan, Vladimir Propp, and Joseph Campbell.[2] The most detailed of these treatments was that of Lord Raglan, who in *The Hero* analyzed the tales of twenty-one heroes and gods to arrive at a twenty-two point outline.[3] The material for these surveys is drawn almost exclusively from Indo-European sources (Campbell's *The Hero with a Thousand Faces* has a wider scope), and students of primitive literature may criticize them because they do not include, and in many cases are inapplicable to, American and West Pacific mythologies. Classicists on

9

the other hand may deplore the neglect of such characteristic Greek heroes as Achilles and Odysseus, may doubt the advisability of grouping gods and heroes together in such classifications, and may question the validity of generalizations based on a wide variety of Greek authors and a mythological development of over a thousand years. As for the adequate classification of primitive hero types, Greenway is inclined to believe it is an almost impossible task.[4] "A compendium of actors in primitive literature," he says, "is as arbitrary as a compendium of forms, and just as unprofitable. There is an endless diversity of heroes." He admits, however, that "an analysis of late folk and early sophisticated heroes is profitable in understanding the primitive archetypes."

For the comparative treatment of the tales of a single author, Pindar, with a sampling of Indian tales such as will be attempted in this survey, the simple outlines of Thompson or of Katherine Spencer[5] with such topics as Birth of Hero, Tasks, Friendly Animals, and the like, will give adequate starting points for the discussion.

BIRTH OF HERO AND HERO TASKS

A first glance at the topics Thompson has listed as characteristic of hero tales among the North American Indians—supernatural birth of the hero, threatening influences in his youth, his rapid growth to maturity, his assignment to dangerous quests, and his encounters with monstrous animals—shows that some of Pindar's heroes, Perseus, Jason, Achilles, and, above all, Heracles, seem to fit the requirements well. There are the remarkable begettings—Perseus and Heracles in golden showers—the swift night journey to save the infant Jason, the extraordinary strength of the baby Heracles and the youth Achilles, taskmasters, Kings Eurystheus, Polydectes, Pelias, and the confrontations with lion, Gorgon, and hundred-foot dragon.

But a closer examination of these large patterns with the motifs of the Indian tales Thompson has assembled reveals significant differences. The gains, or rather the changes, are in reasonableness and refinement, as would seem natural. Here is no Blood-Clot Boy, or birth from wounds or tears or mucus, or child discovered in a salmon's belly, but a golden shower referred to allusively at the begetting of Perseus (the gold snowfall at the visit of Zeus to Alcmene is perhaps an echo)—no instantaneous growth to maturity, but healthy human babies gifted with unusual strength, like Heracles or Achilles, who can strangle the snakes sent by Hera or run down the fleetest of animals without help of hounds. In the Indian tale "Lodge-Boy and Thrown-Away,"[6] the wicked Red Woman kills a pregnant wife and throws away her unborn twins—one behind the tepee-curtain, the other in a spring, and from these places the two presently emerge, able to talk and walk. Jason, wrapped in purple garments, is spirited away at dead of night from the hostile home of Pelias and given to Chiron to rear.[7] Closer parallels are in the taskmasters—usually relatives of the hero in the Indian tales, where uncles or fathers-in-law are often hostile: Pelias is Jason's cousin (in Pindar); Eurystheus, Heracles' cousin; Polydectes, Perseus' stepfather after the marriage he forced on Danaë. The Sun father-in-law in one of the Indian tales offers a curiously close parallel to Aeëtes, son of Helius. The cruel stepmother, who, according to Thompson,[8]

11

appears in folktales more often than any other cruel relative, is not present in the Indian tales, at least in Thompson's summaries, but she may be recognized in *Nemean* I.38 in the person of Hera, who sends the snakes to destroy the baby Heracles in his bed. Phrixus, too, was rescued by the golden-fleeced ram from his stepmother's weapons (*Pyth.* IV. 162). In all these instances the death or removal of the hero is the prime motivation.

In oral storytelling the setting of three tasks, often graded to a climax of difficulty, is a familiar motif that gives needed strength to a construction often loose and rambling. Twice in the Odes of Pindar this primitive patterning[9] seems to show through—once in the story of Bellerophon (*Ol.* XIII. 87-90), where the hero's exploits against the Amazons, the Chimera, and the Solymi are listed in succession (an echo of a similar listing in *Iliad* VI. 179 ff.), and again in the praise of Peleus' feats (*Nem.* III. 33-35), i.e., the cutting of a "matchless" spear, capturing Iolcus single-handed, and the winning of the sea nymph Thetis. Though a threefold enumeration is a common enough rhetorical device to appear anywhere without special comment, the folktale aura which surrounds these early exploits of Peleus forms some justification for considering it a special folktale feature here.[10] Though occasionally the pattern of three appears in the Indian tales, the number four is the great favorite. Perhaps the Indians' strong awareness of the four points of the compass may account for this preference. Over and over again in the Indian tales the pattern emerges—in the Fourth World, in a buffalo cow's attacks, in an identification test which must be four times repeated.[11] Some tightness of construction and orderliness is thus obtained.

Dangerous quests and testings are, of course, *de rigueur* in the hero tale. They are found in Indian tales of every culture area, according to Thompson *(The Folktale,* p. 341), and the most popular kind of quest is that after dangerous animals which may be expected to kill the hero. The animals in American Indian tales are distinguished chiefly by size—an enormous fish which swallows people whole and which the hero must fight from within its belly, a giant clam, a giant serpent, a huge elk whose body becomes a mountain range, and ferocious gulls, dogs, and bears. Other hostile creatures are snakes and otters *(The Folktale,* pp. 331-338 *passim).* Though giant size characterizes some of the Greek monsters of Pindar (the Nemean Lion, for example, and the dragon Jason slays, "vaster than a penteconter"), grotesqueness of shape renders many of them strange and picturesque—the snaky-haired Gorgon, the Chimera belching flames, hundred-headed Cerberus and Typhon, and the brazen-footed bulls that breathe fire. Do these fantastic creatures indicate an imaginative power the Indians do not manifest? Many critics say they have been borrowed from the East;[12] Rose *(Mythology,* p. 31) remarks: "It is not surprising, considering how little the Greeks liked monstrosities, that these products of an imagination not their own are [often] represented as living in the lower world." He mentions the collection of them at the very entrance to Hades in Vergil's *Aeneid* and comments: "They are rather horrors lurking in the background than clear-cut figures of the generally sunny Hellenic mythology." He earlier says, "In all this hideous brood we may safely recognize the influence of non-Greek fancy, chiefly Anatolian, on the Greek mind. The many-membered creatures, Geryon, Kerberos, and the

Hydra, all remind us of the many-armed and many-headed deities of Indian and other Oriental religions. The Chimaira, a composite of lion, goat and dragon . . . suggest[s] the winged, human-headed bulls and other monsters of Assyrian and Babylonian art and legend."

The closeness of animal and human worlds is everywhere apparent in the Indian tales, not only in the person of the hero, who can appear as easily as Coyote, Raven, or Hare as in his human form, but also in the ferocious animals he encounters, for they often have the power of speech and reason, avenging themselves on the person who sent the hero to capture them. This humanizing of the animal world will appear again in the treatment of the Animal Helper theme. It is a feature appearing not at all in Pindar, and rarely in Greek mythology as it has survived, and must be considered as belonging to a very primitive stratum of thought. The monsters subdued were, to the common-sense Greeks, beasts and nothing more. Can one imagine the Nemean Lion or the Hydra pleading with Heracles, as, for example, Fafnir pleads with Sigurth in the *Fafnismol* of the Norse Edda? Generalizations, however, are dangerous. The Sphinx certainly had the power of speech as well as "human" feelings of humiliation and hatred when her riddle was guessed; even the monster Typhon, whom Hesiod describes in such grotesque detail, had at times "speech which the gods understand" (*Theogony*, 831), and the Python (according to Hyginus, *Fab.* CXL), learning from an oracle that a son of Leto would cause his death, pursued the pregnant goddess to destroy her. Traces of this humanization may be seen perhaps in the fact that elaborate genealogies of the monsters, as in the *Theogony* of Hesiod, were often devised. Pindar shows such interest only twice in the Odes, once in speaking of the parentage of the Gorgons (Graeae?) and again in terming Pegasus the offspring of Medusa (*Pyth.* XII. 13; *Ol.* XIII. 63).[13]

It has often been remarked that animal adversaries predominate in the Twelve Labors of Heracles, and that such contests may be considered the earliest of the cycle, and earlier than those of other heroes, Perseus perhaps excepted. Nilsson, for example, states: "Such exploits [of killing or capturing wild animals] are really quite primitive in character, much more primitive than the fighting through which Homeric heroes gain fame and glory."[14] Heracles starts early on such encounters, as we have seen, grappling when but an infant with the snakes Hera sent to destroy him. Farnell says, "There is every reason for supposing that this remarkable story of the amazing infant had never been recorded, at least in high poetry, before."[15] It belonged to genuine Theban folklore, and may have inspired, in Wilamowitz' estimation, coinage of Boeotia which was to be followed by that of Cnidos and Cyzicus.[16] As for the Labors themselves, Pindar refers to five of them: the Nemean Lion (often in connection with the founding of the Nemean Games), the "savage hounds" of Geryon,[17] the flesh-eating mares of Diomedes, the golden-horned deer, and Cerberus, and there are several general references to "beasts he overcame on land and sea," among which may have been the dragon that threatened Laomedon's Troy.[18] Monsters are much more prominent in non-Homeric than in Homeric tradition, according to the Chadwicks, who cite the stories of Perseus, Heracles, and Theseus. "It may be observed," they remark, "that in most of these adventures the hero is unaccompanied, that the scene is often laid in distant

15

lands, and that they all relate to times anterior to the siege of Troy."[19]

The early hero might have giants or ogres, as well as ferocious beasts, to contend with. Indian tales show much variety and fanciful imagination: there is a sucking monster, a cliff ogre who pushes his victims off a precipice, sharp-elbowed women, burr-women who cling to the hero's back as does the Old Man of the Sea, a sort of female Polyphemus in the person of a cannibal giantess, women who wrestle on knife-filled straw or who challenge to dangerous swinging contests, an old woman pot-tilter whose pot sucks its victims into boiling water as she points it at them, and most striking of all, an ogre with sandals of fire who treads a circle of flame around his enemies. That the hero's adversaries are often female, as the list above shows, is a marked Indian characteristic.[20]

In this respect Greek hero tales differ widely. There are few "proper" witches (Circe? the Graeae?) in Greek mythology, though, to the disparagement of the fair sex, the many composite monsters—Harpies, Sirens, Gorgons, the Sphinx, the Echidna, the Hydra, the Chimera—are invariably female. As for the Odes of Pindar, the human opponents of the heroes are all male, with the exception of the Amazons, those "brazen-bowed, horse-riding" warriors, whom other heroes beside Heracles encountered—Peleus and Bellerophon in Pindar, Theseus elsewhere. If one wished a striking contrast between these handsome warriors and the ugly and malicious hags of Indian mythology, it is here at hand. For the rest, the single human adversaries in Pindar are those of Heracles (perhaps because his adventures go back to very early times), and a motley assembly they make. Many of them are sons of gods—Cycnus, son of Ares, who once subdued Heracles himself; Antaeus, the Libyan giant, who challenged strangers to a wrestling match and roofed his father Poseidon's temple with their skulls; Geryon, the ogre of the west, whose cattle Heracles stole; the "haughty" twin Moliones, sons of Poseidon; and above all, the herdsman Alcyoneus, "huge as a mountain," who had once destroyed by casting an enormous stone twelve chariots and their twenty-four occupants when Heracles led a force against him. Porphyrion, King of the Giants, whom Heracles helped Apollo slay in the battle of the gods and giants, has a place here, too.[21] Nilsson (*Greek Folk Religion*, p. 57) is of the opinion that such struggles against "highwaymen and robbers" are late in comparison with struggles with beasts and monsters—he is referring here to Theseus' so-called Labors in comparison with those of Heracles. The statement probably holds true for the developing stories of Heracles, he also believes.[22] In many of Pindar's brief allusions the picturesque details which were no doubt known to his audience do not appear, such as the triple bodies of Geryon, the double-joined form of the Moliones, the invulnerability of Cycnus, who roofed the temple of Apollo with the skulls of his victims, nor are Heracles' methods of dealing with the ogres specified—his lifting Antaeus from the earth to strangle him, or hurling back Alcyoneus' magic rock to cause the giant's death.[23] Bacchylides is much more explicit in narrating the similar exploits of Theseus—with Sinis, the Fir Bender, Sciron, the cliff ogre, Periphetes with the iron club, and the famous Procrustes, with his adjustable bed.[24]

Besides the capturing or killing of wild animals and conflicts with ogres, the Indian tales present countless

17

other tests for their heroes—a variety of athletic contests such as swimming, diving, tree-pulling, climbing, harpooning, tobogganing, and such homely, everyday ones as staying awake, eating (the food offered is often burning or poisonous), delousing, as well as simple abandonment and imprisonment.[25] One would have to search far in Greek writers to find such variety, but there will be mention of an eating contest later,[26] and Heracles' fifth Labor—the Cleansing of the Augean Stables—has the homely touch of true folklore, whether he performed the task by the magic of reversing a broom, as the hero does in the Norse tale of Mastermaid, or by the trick of turning rivers to clear out the dung.[27] Jason must perform an "ordinary" task of plowing, but the poet raises it in dignity to a superhuman feat—he was to plow with bulls that breathe fire, and the depth of the furrow was to be a "full fathom." The theft of the girdle of the Amazon Queen by Heracles might give opportunity for humorous folklore treatment.

When we come to the Cercopes, whom Heracles also encountered, we are indeed close to folklore material. These mischievous dwarfs, during the hero's servitude to Queen Omphale, once pestered him so that he hung them upside down from a pole and carried them off. *Fragment* 161 of Pindar apparently refers to this incident: "They were bound with fetters head downward" —a line which recalls the relief on an archaic metope at Selinus, which Pindar might have seen.[28] Warned by their mother Theia to beware of "Blackbottom," they realized from this upside-down position that they had already met him, and their jokes at his expense made Heracles laugh in turn and release them.[29] A burlesque poem, three lines of which have been preserved, attributed to Homer by Zenobius, tells of their wandering mischievous career. They were eventually turned into stones or into apes.[30] It seems clear that they were folk-tale figures somewhat similar to the two Ahaiyute, who constantly ventured forth against the warnings of their grandmother, slew monsters, played tricks on old women, and laughed and joked through it all.[31] The scatological flavor of the Cercopes' story reminds one again of some Indian tales where excrement offers an opportunity for humor.[32]

There are two particularly striking tests for the Indian heroes—passing through snapping doors which "try to bite" and going under malevolent trees which swoop down upon the passerby and kill him.[33] For the former, Pindar's Clashing Islands in the fourth *Pythian* furnish a parallel, though one immeasurably superior in romantic beauty. These islands through which the *Argo* must pass, the poet describes as alive, though after the passing of the marvelous ship they "stood still in death."[34] Pindar is the first to suggest that the rocks were "alive,"[35] and the animistic origin of this idea seems clear. That the rocks became stationary after the *Argo* passed is a post-Homeric tradition.[36] A similar feature in Greek mythology concerns the Sirens—their power was ended once a ship had successfully passed their islands. In the Indian tale "Lodge-Boy and Thrown-Away," the swooping trees had their branches broken and were unable to rise again after the boys had jumped over them.[37] This is the Unique Exception motif (Z 300).

"I would take my revenge on you, if I had the power!" angry Achilles once cried to Apollo, when the god deceived him and led him away from the wall of

Troy.[38] So the spirit of a hero might even lead him to engage in contest with a god. "Homer's moderation forbade him to allow his heroes to venture too far," Bowra says in his *Heroic Poetry*,[39] although in the *Iliad* Diomede wounds both Ares and Aphrodite, and in the *Odyssey* Menelaus strives successfully with the sea-god Proteus.[40] Such struggles of heroes with gods, in the words of Webster, "belong to an age when divine kings could meet and rout divinities."[41] Nilsson, too, speaks of the "old trait" appearing in Homer's tale that Heracles wounded Hera in the breast, and also wounded Hades. In the goddess Dione's words, Heracles is shown as a "rough, violent man who did not shrink from shameful deeds, even distressing with his darts the gods who hold Olympus." "The Homeric poet," continues Nilsson, "is unable to understand how a mortal man can dare to raise weapons against a god."[42] Even so late an author as Pindar mentions three such encounters of his favorite hero Heracles (with Poseidon, Apollo, and Hades). The critics are divided on the interpretation of this passage, the most natural being that the poet rejects the stories as impossible:

> "For how could Heracles
>   Have brandished a club in his hands against the
>   trident,
>   When Poseidon stood over Pylos and drove on him,
>   And Phoebus drove, shaking his silver bow?
>   Nor did Death keep the rod unshaken
>   With which he brings down
>   The bodies of men to the hollow street of the dying.
>   Fling this tale away, my lips!"

> (*Ol.* IX. 29-36, translated by Bowra.)

Parallels among the Indian tales are hard to find and difficult to assess, for there often seems no clear-cut distinction between supernatural beings (gods?) and mortals. Lowie shows the fluid state of such conceptions in his discussion of the "test theme" in North American mythology. "The scope of the celestial," he says, "is seen to coincide with that of human activities. The Sun is a cannibal, an abductor of children, the transformer, the husband of a frog, the marked-dog husband. He may in different versions of the same tale act as the cruel father-in-law and as the hero's abettor; he is tester as well as tested hero."[43] One can adduce, of course, such tales as those of the Sun Snarer, and the war against the destructive south wind, described as a gigantic bird (the hero reduces its force by breaking its wing), but sun and wind here are apparently not conceived of as deities.[44] If one wished in Greek mythology to come closer to the Indian conception, one might think of Achilles' fight with the River Scamander, or better still, of Heracles' threat, when once oppressed by the sun's heat, to shoot him with his bow.[45] A Tlingit tale, from the northwest coast of America, tells of a boy who shot an arrow at a star which immediately darkened, and Greenway in his *Primitive Reader* gives a Miao story from southwestern China—"The Fearful Sun"—which contains the sun-shooting motif.[46] If, on the contrary, one wished to cite a primitive example of a contest more in the Greek fashion between a clearly conceived god and man, there is the African Luyi tale which Mrs. Feldmann calls "singularly dramatic": the god Nyambe is forced to flee and climb up the sky rope when men attempt to kill him.[47]

21

JOURNEYS OF HERO

One of the common exploits of the hero is an expedition to the Underworld. Gilgamesh ventured there in the Babylonian epic, Vainamoinen in the *Kalevala,* Odysseus in the *Odyssey*.[48] There are several stories of this kind among the Indian tales, some of which have a remarkable likeness to the Orpheus story of Greek mythology. Such are the ones entitled "The Man Who Brought His Wife back from Spiritland," "Orpheus," and "Coyote and Eagle Visit the Land of the Dead."[49] In the heroic tales of Pindar where victorious achievement is stressed, there is little room for such themes, which are often those of frustration and disillusion. One of the Odes of Bacchylides (V) does describe the meeting of Heracles with Meleager in the Lower World, and Pindar may have treated a similar visit in a dithyramb (II) entitled "The Descent of Heracles, or Cerberus." The story of the hero's wounding of Hades, apparently a well-known tale, the poet may mention only to reject, as we have seen, but a direct treatment of the Harrying of Hell theme does not appear in the extant Odes.[50]

Besides journeys to the Land of the Dead other venturings to distant remarkable lands occur in the North American Indian tales—journeys to the Sky for star husbands, to the Sun's house, to the underwater worlds of beaver and deer; and there is one highly imaginative exploring of the Land of Shadows, where Chief Echo presided and the inhabitants lived on the odors of food.[51] The Irish seem particularly fond of journeys to the Land of Youth; and the tale of Oisin, who was taken on a white steed by the beautiful Nia of the golden hair to Tir-na-n-og, where gold and silver, honey and wine were

in abundance, is a charming example.[52] It is tempting
to see in the Hyperborean Land, which Pindar several
times refers to, a similar Land of Youth. *Fragment* 272
(Bowra) describes the inhabitants as living for a thousand years,[53] and in the earliest of the Odes (*Pythian* X)
the poet vividly sketches a picture of their land where
feasting and dancing and the music of lyre and flute de-
lighted these happy bay-crowned people, who knew
neither old age nor toil. Perseus went there, with Athena
for his guide, on his way to slay the Gorgon. Heracles,
too (Pindar's account is unique here), seems to have
paid them two visits, once for the golden-horned hind,
and again (this time quite against ecological probabilities) to procure olive trees to plant in the newly established precinct of Zeus at Olympia (*Ol.* III. 13, 33).
"Neither by foot nor by ship can one make one's way by
the marvelous road to the Hyperboreans" (*Pyth.* X. 29-
30), and with this sentence these blissful people are
placed definitely in the land of faërie. Or if we care to
look farther for parallels, we may find one in the
story "The Northern Lights" (a tale of the Wabanaki
Indians of northern New England),[54] in which Chief
Morning Star, in search of his son, visited a country far
to the north, lighted only by a peculiar glow, where a
strange tribe who played ball on a many-colored play-
ground entertained him. After this hospitality the old
chief and his son returned on birds along the Milky Way
—this last detail suggesting the shamanistic journeys
through the air attributed to the Hyperborean seer,
Abaris. *Fragment* 270 of Pindar mentions Abaris as
contemporary with Croesus, though there is no reference
to his "soul-flights" or to the famous golden arrow which
he carried or rode on his journeys.[55]

WAR

With the theme of war we move away from the oral folktales Thompson discusses into the realm of legend, and must do without Indian counterparts. The old Greek mythology knew of great wars against Troy and against Thebes, which break the sequence of fanciful "metal" Ages in Hesiod's *Works and Days*.[56] These wars are mentioned frequently in the Odes, the long siege of Troy for its fame established by Homer and the first war against Thebes with Adrastus and Amphiaraus as its heroes, treated naturally enough in the work of a Theban poet. By means of these wars Pindar bridges the chronological gap between the more remote mythological adventures and the celebration of contemporary athletic victories—his real subject matter. Among his heroes Peleus and Heracles serve this purpose admirably, since their lives span both early and late adventures. Peleus—an early folklore figure who captures Iolcus single-handed, journeys with Jason for the Fleece, and wins a sea-goddess for his bride—is brought nearer the present by his aid to Heracles in the first Trojan War. Heracles, too, that ubiquitous hero, has adventures in both early and late periods.[57] So Pindar, while retaining the marvels of faërie and the splendors of the heroic past, links both to the deeds of his victorious athletes in one high mood of glorious achievement.

FRIENDLY ANIMALS

Thompson comments on the closeness of the animal and human worlds in folktales everywhere. "We easily move from one to the other," he says, "hardly noticing when the transition is made. In the European nursery tales, the wolf talks to Red Ridinghood, the cat and dog help the hero recover magic objects or the frog marries the princess."[58] Andrew Lang, many years before, had characterized the incidents of popular tales with similar words: "Talking beasts are common, beasts acting as men are common: no less common, among savages, is the frame of mind in which practically no distinction is taken between gods, beasts, and men. . . . The more civilised the people, the less of these elements appears in their ritual, usage, and myth: most survives in their popular tales, and even in these it is gradually miti-gated."[59] This closeness of animal and human is a strik-ing feature of the Indian tales. The culture hero espe-cially is often conceived in animal form, though the nature of his achievements shows that he is at the same time given human characteristics. So Manabozho ap-pears in the Central Woodland as the White Rabbit, and his brother as Wolf; Mink and Blue Jay play his role on the North Pacific coast. In the Trickster tales the hero may appear in animal shape like Coyote or Porcupine; he may quickly transform himself into fish or other creature, and friendly animals often come to his assist-ance.[60]

The Helpful Animal motif is a popular one in folk-tales of all nations, as a glance at the Thompson *Motif-Index* will show. In the Indian tales under discussion the hero is once helped by a lizard that lets him mas-querade in his coat and by a gopher that gnaws a tunnel under a giant elk the hero is to kill. A bat, with a magic basket made of spider web, helps him escape from the nest of a giant eagle; a mouse helps gnaw the net in which the sun is caught, and, a unique example from the tales of the Southwest, a friendly insect on the hero's head "substitutes" by smoking an otherwise fatal pipe.[61]

That animals played a correspondingly important role in early Greek tales seems a reasonable assumption, though ancient oral literature, in which such material might occur, is of course unrecorded. Significant evidence may be gathered, however, from scattered references, in one instance from the tale of Cupid and Psyche in Apuleius, considered by Halliday to represent one of the few genuine oral tales from classical antiquity.[62] In this tale a helpful ant summons all her friends to assist Psyche in the task of sorting grain. An eagle also comforts her and brings her a flask of the deadly water she was ordered to procure from the sources of the Styx.[63] Quite a collection of speaking birds may be gathered, among them the chattering crows in the *Argonautica* of Apollonius that suggested to Mopsus the wisdom of leaving Jason alone for his appeal to Medea.[64] Then there are the "oracular animals" that lead to Thebes, to Troy, to Aegeae. Arion, the "speaking horse" of Adrastus, is another example,[65] though the paternity of the horse—the god Poseidon himself—helps to explain his unusual nature. That the gods in many tales transform themselves into animals may in a similar way be considered survival of early kinds of belief. But apart from these divine examples the gap between such primitive conceptions and the Greek hero tale is extraordinarily wide; one has only to think of the shock one experiences when Achilles' horse in the *Iliad* suddenly speaks out, to realize how far from the primitive world of talking animals the world of Homer is.[66] In Pindar the horse Arion does not appear, though his master Adrastus has a conspicuous role. Pegasus, the winged steed of Bellerophon, might qualify as a "survival," and better yet, the ram with the golden fleece which bore Phrixus away from danger, but in both these cases the animals do not act in their own persons, so to speak, but are mute and directed by the gods. The ram is miraculously provided, and Pegasus is tamed by Athena's golden bridle;[67] so the wonder or irrationality is explained, just as in Homer the phenomenon of the speaking horse is explained by the agency of Hera.

A curious instance of Pindar's rejection of the use of a speaking bird may be seen in his handling of the story of Coronis. The scholiast reports the story as told by Hesiod in his *Eoiae:* a tattling crow told Apollo of the faithlessness of Coronis, who had pledged herself to him. In Pindar's account the god sensed her infidelity "by his consciousness alone"—a clear rejection of the common version, in Bowra's opinion.[68] It is not the credibility of the tale that Pindar apparently rejects—greater wonders appear without comment in the Odes—but he evidently thinks the omniscience of the god is impugned and slighted.

Related to the Friendly Animal motif is the motif of the animal nurse, often associated with the childhood of heroes. The most famous example perhaps is the Romulus and Remus story, one of two animal tales which, as Thompson says, have had extensive migrations.[69] No instances of this motif appear in Thompson's summaries, but in his *Tales* themselves they may be found. In tales from the Mackenzie River district and from the Plains, hare, beaver, and crow take the part.[70]

In Greek mythology the theme of the Friendly Animal has survived surprisingly well. Hyginus CCLII gives a summary of such stories, the animals concerned being deer, goat, heifer, mare, bitch, and she-wolf in stories of both late and early dates. The motif was often associated with that of child-exposure, and since this last was a favorite theme, especially in Greek comedy, the subordinate motif may owe its long life to this association. An example may be found in the Odes of Pindar—the serpents who feed the infant Iamus honey instead of their usual poisonous venom (*Ol.* VI. 45 [78b]). The explanation of this violation of nature is the usual one—the direct agency of the gods, stressed by the scholiast on the passage. One wonders whether the many stories of bees resting on the lips of children destined for greatness—Stesichorus, Aeschylus, Plato, Pindar himself—like the story of the doves which protected the baby Horace with leaves, may be poetical survivals of this theme.

Another instance of this motif in Pindar, disguised, it is true, may be that of the Centaur Chiron, the "divine beast," to whom baby Jason is taken, and who is shown as the tutor of the child Achilles. Why Thetis did not see fit to raise her child herself Pindar does not divulge. Instruction in philosophy, medicine, and hunting would seem justification for youthful training, but the words Pindar uses are those of infant care, and one suspects here a trace of the folklore story of the offended sea-bride who abandoned her offspring in anger at the breaking of some tabu by her mortal husband.[71] In all these rather blurred instances of animal motifs in Pindar, the tone has been raised by the poet from the primitive or childish level by touches of beauty or wonder. We are shown the "thick-fleeced ram of gold," winged Pegasus soaring "in the lonely spaces of the sky," the gray-eyed serpents feeding the child honey as he lay wrapped in saffron garments on beds of purple flowers, instead of the homely spider, or beaver, or crow of the Indian tales.

MAGIC AND MAGICAL POWERS

Magic and magical powers of all sorts form a very considerable part of folktale motifs, as is evident from the summary Thompson gives of them in *The Folktale*.[72] Here are automatic saws, self-filling purses, table cloths producing food, magic stones and rings, self-moving boats, magic mills and pots, traveling caps, horns and whistles to summon soldiers, magic herbs and salves, as well as mention of the power of self-transformation, the power to move through the air or under water, resuscitation of the dead and the like—all gathered from world-wide collections of folktales.

The magic objects of the Indian societies we are considering are not often hand-made or elaborately devised as many of the objects in the paragraph above, but are often such simple things as stretching trees, spider-web ropes, and spruce cones which may form a forest. The power of self-transformation is especially frequent: the hero, especially Trickster, may transform himself at a moment's notice into ant, tree, dish, eagle, fish, or bird. He may be swallowed by a fish and survive, and then proceed to resuscitate other victims of the same imprisonment. He may enter into contests in magic, have ability to cure or beautify himself and to control the weather. Over fifty examples of this kind may be easily gathered from Thompson's pages, making the practice of magic perhaps the most striking characteristic of these Indian tales.

That the Greeks in general had passed through this phase, "relegating it to an unimportant corner," is

Bowra's contention in *The Greek Experience.* There still were "elements of miracle and marvel," he continues, "but it is noteworthy that these are nearly always the direct work of the gods."[73] Elsewhere he draws a clear distinction between what he calls "shamanistic poetry" and "heroic poetry." In shamanistic poetry magic is predominant; heroic poetry concentrates, "not on a man's magical powers, but on his specifically human virtues."[74] And this may express succinctly the chief difference between the Indian hero tales we have been considering and the treatment of Pindar, in whom the spirit of the Greek epic still lived. The power of self-transformation may be taken as a touchstone: Trickster and Blood-Clot Boy have it—Homer's and Pindar's heroes not at all. If one wished to make adequate comparison with the Indian tales, the transformations effected by the gods would have to be considered. The hero in Pindar usually performs his tasks by direct confrontation and sheer physical strength, and suitably so, since the Odes exalt the very real strength of the victors in the Games.

But Pindar, curiously enough, seems attracted to two tales in which magic is predominant—the stories of Perseus and Jason—the two which many critics feel to be nearest to genuine folktales. In four of the Odes the adventures of Perseus are referred to, and the Argonautic Expedition is the subject for one of the lengthiest of Pindar's mythical narratives. As unified tale-types both of these will be discussed later (p. 92); here the question of magical aid to the hero is the chief consideration. That Pindar somewhere referred to the winged sandals and the pouch for the Gorgon's head (the *kibisis*), a statement in Apollodorus (II. 4. 2) seems to indicate. His name is joined there with that of Hesiod, who in the *Shield of Heracles* described Perseus, equipped with sandals, pouch, and cap of darkness, in full flight from the Gorgons after the slaying of their sister Medusa. Bowra numbers this reference *Fr.* 269; Snell, more conservatively, omits it, probably because he can cite no actual words of Pindar to which to tie the reference, though the whole story was a very early one, widely known no doubt in Pindar's day. Halliday devotes an entire chapter (VI) to the Perseus story in his *Indo-European Folk-Tales and Greek Legend,* and his conclusions about the magic paraphernalia of the hero are summarized briefly here. "For the student of folktale," he says (pp. 135-37 *passim*), "the occurrence of the magical objects in this very early tale is of the greatest interest, for throughout the Indo-European area they figure prominently in a number of stories. . . . The shoes of swiftness in the form of winged sandals are elsewhere characteristic of Hermes" (who was early the supernatural helper for Perseus, later to be ousted from chief place by Athena). The cap of darkness or helmet of Hades appeared as early as Homer, worn by Athena in the battle at Troy (*Iliad* V. 845). The *kibisis*, or wallet, for carrying the Gorgon's head, is the most interesting part of Perseus' equipment, since the word is not Greek. Halliday thinks the motif is of Eastern (Anatolian?) origin, perhaps an adaptation of the *Tischen-deck-dich* of the Märchen, a table which at the word of command magically produces food. Cap, shoes, and wallet form the chief part of the equipment of Hesiod's Perseus and belong to the original story. They are procured from the Graeae (hags whose one "community" eye Perseus steals), or from the Nymphs (named

Neides on early vase-paintings) to whom the blinded Graeae direct the hero.

These points all have bearing on a difficult passage of Pindar (*Pyth*. XII. 7-21)—a passage in which Pindar condenses much of the Perseus story, though his real interest at this point seems to be in explaining how Athena invented a kind of flute music. She was inspired, the poet says, as she listened to the hissing of the snakes on the Gorgon's head "the time he [Perseus] slew the third of those sisters, bringing doom to sea-girt Seriphus and its folk. In truth he blinded [baffled?] the strange offspring of Phorcus [Graeae? Gorgons?] and made bitter to Polydectes the bridal gift and the long enslavement and forced marriage of the mother." If we translate the verb "blinded" (a rather late meaning), the reference is of course to the stealing of the Graeae's one eye; if "baffled," the reference might be either to this trick or to the wearing of the cap of darkness which prevented the sister Gorgons from tracking Perseus as he fled. Both Gorgons and Graeae were the offspring of Phorcus, though the term is more often applied to the Graeae than to their snaky-haired relatives. The "bridal-gift" is of course the head of Medusa Perseus had promised to bring; the "doom" that befell Polydectes and all the Seriphians, that of being turned into stone by the head of Medusa, a most effective weapon. Burton says of this passage in *Pythian* XII that its ambiguities may never be resolved but that if we fill the gaps, all the paraphernalia of the saga lurk there. Bowra says an actual shaman "may perhaps be seen in Perseus, who flies on winged sandals, wears a cap of darkness, and kills the Gorgon with the help of a magic mirror."[75]

As for the tale of the Argonauts, the salve to anoint

Jason against the flames of the fire-breathing bulls and the charm given him by Medea to calm the dragon are fully in the folklore tradition. The knife of Daedalus, given to Peleus, was apparently a magic knife, though no use is made of its properties by the poet.[76] We should add, too, from another tale, the magic bridle which Bellerophon uses to tame Pegasus. But note that Athena gives this bridle to Bellerophon; she is present when Perseus confronts the Gorgon; and it is Aphrodite who furnishes the magic iynx to inspire Medea with love for Jason. In *Olympian* I Poseidon gives winged steeds and a chariot of gold to Pelops.[77]

Apart from such equipment provided by the gods, the weapons of Pindar's heroes, though often extraordinary, are non-magical. Peleus cuts his own huge spear[78] (in the *Iliad* it was a gift of Chiron), perhaps the very spear that later his son Achilles used against Memnon (*Nem.* VI. 54-55). Pindar does not describe it in his last passage except to call it "very wrathful," but the scholiast says that it was remarkable in having a double point, and was therefore doubly deadly. The adjective "very wrathful," he adds, recalls phrases in Homer: spears are there sometimes described "as eager to glut themselves" on the flesh of foes, as if they shared the feelings of the one who cast them. These examples may show nothing but the poet's desire for vividness, yet back of them may lie a suggestion of folk-belief in the actual personality of the weapon: the "angry" or "vengeful" sword is a definite motif in English and Scottish popular ballads.[79]

According to tradition, Heracles fashioned his famous club from an uprooted tree. Though Pindar does not mention this accomplishment, the club appears in sev-

33

eral passages, with the devastating effects of its blows vividly shown. The bow and arrows are mentioned twice, once in the hero's battle with the Giants, and again in connection with the story of Philoctetes and the prophecy that bound them with the fall of Troy.[80] More stress is put on the skin of the Nemean Lion, which Heracles used for protective covering. Wearing this huge pelt the hero, as he stands in the courtyard of Telamon on his errand to enlist his aid in the war against Laomedon, makes a prayer to Zeus in behalf of the yet unborn son of his friend: "May he grow to be as hardy as the skin of this huge beast!" The skin is usually described as impenetrable—Heracles must kill the lion by strangling it, but Farnell praises the poet's moderation here: "The idea of the toughness of the skin was degraded by later littérateurs to a magical significance, but Pindar, like Homer, keeps the high humanity of his heroes aloof from magic."[81] The appearance of the eagle, however, at the close of Heracles' prayer the poet accepts as a valid confirmatory sign—"After the name of the bird you will call him the mighty Ajax"—and we have here a suggestion of the belief in "name-magic." *Nomen-omen* is the concise way of putting it.[82]

Rhys Carpenter, in mentioning Homer's indifference to magic (he is speaking of the magic plant which Hermes gives to Odysseus to protect him against Circe's powers, and which the poet apparently forgets to have Odysseus use), deplores, as he puts it, "the classic Greek's failure to comprehend faërie,"[83] but compensation for lack of supernatural accomplishments may be made in heroic poetry by amplifying the hero's natural powers. The heroes of Homer and Pindar are given extraordinary strength. Achilles in Homer can wield a spear

34

ordinary men could not wield, and drive home the bolt
to his hut which his comrades together could not force
through. Heracles, in Pindar, wrestles with huge beasts,
rears lofty pillars to mark the limits of his adventurings,
and overcomes Alcyoneus "huge as a mountain." Jason
plows a furrow a full fathom deep; Peleus captures
Iolcus single-handed. The Greek heroes usually face
their tasks alone, though occasionally they have squires
like Iolaus for helpers. Iolaus is given full honors in
the Odes, finally avenging by the death of Eurystheus
the tasks imposed by that king on Heracles.[84] Patroclus
took this place as the squire of Achilles in the *Iliad*, and
in Pindar a similar relationship between the friends is
indicated in several passages.[85] The motif of the Extraordinary Companions in the story of the Argonauts is
not fully utilized by the poet.

The equipment of the Indian hero is usually simple;
he has magic power at his command constantly, and so
does not need specialized weapons, though caps or robes
of invisibility and magic canoes and arrows occasionally
appear.[86] As for helpers, in one tale an old woman gives
him a bladder full of cold wind to enable him to endure
the heat of the sun; in another, magic tobacco is provided by his wife, or he may pick up playthings of his
brothers when he starts out on his adventures—a knife,
some eagle down, a sour cranberry—which prove helpful
later on. His grandmother may give him weapons—a
magic bow, a shinny stick, some sweathouse wood.[87] The
Kindly Grandmother motif is a frequently recurring
one in Indian tales, and, another frequent folktale
motif, the wife or daughter of his opponent often comes
to his aid. Medea has a similar role in the Jason story as
we shall see in a following topic, Winning a Bride.[88]

TRICKERY

Trickery and magic form separate categories in the Thompson *Motif-Index,* but it is evident that they may overlap, for magic, when employed for deception, is certainly a kind of trickery. There are many tricks and deceptions, however, which make no use of magic means, and it is these which now should be added to the discussion.

The delight of child and primitive man in tales of trickery is well known, and Thompson states that the most characteristic feature of the Indian tales he summarizes is the popularity of trickster stories. The trickster in these stories sometimes appears in human form, like the culture hero Manabozho, or, almost interchangeably, as animal and human, like Coyote or Porcupine. His activities frequently have to do with the catching and killing of game. So he entices animals over a precipice, he feigns death in order to catch them, he persuades ducks to dance with their eyes shut and then kills them one by one, he cheats in wrestling and racing matches for the prize, he may even transform himself into a dish to steal the food people place upon it. Self-transformation is, as we have seen, one of his chief methods to escape from his enemies, to seduce women, to delude his prey, and these self-transformations are often fantastic—to a stone, a dead deer, an ant, a ball of eagle's down. The preindustrial society of the Indian world is reflected in the frequent use of natural, not manufactured objects and the preliterate in the absence of verbal tricks such as Odysseus used with his famous "Noman" stratagem. Gluttony and desire for revenge seem to be the chief motivations of the Indian trickster, though for sheer amusement he sometimes plays the numskull or the buffoon.[89]

An extensive study of the Wisconsin Winnebago Trickster Cycle was made in 1956 by Paul Radin. Here a collection of forty-nine episodes delineates fully the Trickster's amatory, game-hunting, scatological, and other escapades.[90] In Part IV of this book Karl Kerényi sums up his impressions: "Between the spider, the trickster of the animal world, and Hermes, the trickster among the gods, stands the trickster of the Winnebago."[91] Greenway comments on the universality of the Trickster character, going back, as he says, to the "oldest written story in the world, the Gilgamesh epic." He names Hercules and Mercury as forms he has assumed; among the North American Indians he includes such figures as Coyote, Raven, Hare, Manabozho, and Wisakedjak; among the newcomers to this country on the slave ships, Brer Rabbit. "There is no form he may not take."[92]

Greece, even in Homer's day, had long outgrown its childhood, as Gilbert Murray showed many years ago in his *Rise of the Greek Epic*,[93] and naive delight in such stories is not often apparent in the tales that survive. There is one instance in a passage of Hesiod's *Works and Days*,[94] which tells of Zeus's display of illiberal humor at the creation of Pandora. The god laughed aloud when he first saw the beguiling creature who was to bring disaster to Prometheus, his adversary. The chivalrous nature of the epic condemns cowardice and actions that imply falseness, lying, cheating, and perjury. "The treason of Pandarus is something which that unfortunate person might have felt shame for had he lived. The poet himself seems a little ashamed of mentioning such behavior on the part of a hero, even a hostile hero, and arranges as usual to lay the real guilt upon a god."[95]

Deceptions practiced by the Greek gods would require a long and separate treatment. Among men, the "professional" tricksters are few—Autolycus, the cattle-lifter, Sisyphus, who cheated Death himself (perhaps the folklore type of the Master Thief, according to Rose),[96] and the "wily Odysseus"—all three connected by curious mythological ties. Autolycus is not very prominent apart from a story of his thefts from Sisyphus; Sisyphus, as early as Homer, is undergoing everlasting punishment; and the character of Odysseus, after Homer, deteriorates rapidly in literature until it reaches its lowest depth in the *Aeneid*.

The infrequency of such motifs in Pindar's Odes reflects in part this general Greek background, in part no doubt his own individual taste. His tales, though many of them date from a remote past, are couched in terms of his own "civilized" day, and are either judged accordingly, or have their cruder features omitted altogether. Of course the appropriateness of selecting heroes renowned for physical prowess rather than for intellectual adroitness is natural in poems which celebrate victories in the great Games. But the poet evidently admired the straightforward courage of the heroes he chose to celebrate—Heracles, Peleus, Castor and Polydeuces for the earlier periods, Ajax, Diomede, and Achilles for the time of the Trojan War. His so-called "anti-Homeric bias"[97] may be partly explained by this preference. The "wily Odysseus" is no favorite of his (the themes of the *Odyssey* are scarcely mentioned in the Odes), and he seems to some critics to blame Homer (actually the "Homer" of the Epic Cycle) for favoring

Odysseus over Ajax in the Contest of Arms.[98] To take another example, the trickery of Thetis in shape-changing to elude Peleus is met, not by opposing magic or by help of the gods, but by sheer hardihood and endurance.[99]

In spite of his small debt to Homeric subject matter, Pindar on the whole preserves in his characters the chivalrous spirit of the Homeric epic.[100] Trickery and deceit, such as the attempts of Tantalus and Coronis to mislead the gods, the treachery of Laomedon, Clytemnestra, and Ixion against their fellow men, are condemned and punished. With regard to some of Pindar's heroes, however, distinctions must be drawn. Heracles' ambush of the Moliones is treated as entirely legitimate, as is Perseus' "baffling" the Graeae and Gorgons:[101] the first may be justified as an act of war and a return for Augeas' treachery, the second explained as quite in keeping with the folktale spirit of the narrative—that it is "honorable to achieve success by trickery." If we are to read behind Pindar's narrative the theft of the eye of the Graeae, a close parallel may be found in the Indian tale of the Deceived Blind Men from the North Pacific area. Thompson notes the similarity, though he disclaims direct influence.[102]

There are omissions, conscious or otherwise, in other well-known stories involving trickery told by Pindar. The theft of Heracles' bow from Philoctetes by "godlike heroes," which Sophocles posed as a serious moral problem in the mind of young Neoptolemus, the poet passes by without judgment, nor is there any reference in the account of Pelops' race with Oenomaus to Myrtilus' treachery to his master, or to Pelops' treachery to Myrtilus after the race. Indeed the implication of Pindar's

39

words is that the victory was gained by the divine steeds alone.[103] Again, the "real and not very reputable cause" of the fight of the Dioscuri with Idas and Lynceus—cattle stealing?—"Pindar glosses over," as Bowra says, "to acquit the Dioscuri of any imputation of wrongdoing" and to set "them in as favourable a light as possible."[104] It is dangerous, of course, in view of Pindar's habit of condensation, to make too positive judgments on omissions from well-known stories.[105]

The question of trickery (apart from warfare) with regard to Heracles poses some interesting questions. We have seen that Greenway places this hero along with Hermes as typical examples in his list of "universal" tricksters. But Kerényi, commenting on Radin's Winnebago Trickster Cycle, seems reluctant to do so, though he admits there are striking resemblances between Greek and Indian figures. "To judge by what Theophrastus says of character," he declares, "the trickster could hardly be mentioned in the same breath with Heracles, the 'trickless hero with the club.' Yet the impression one gets from the Winnebago stories about the trickster, if one approaches him from the side of Greek mythology, is almost that of encountering an early outwitted, woman-chasing, gluttonous Heracles, rather than a double of the divine trickster of Greek mythology—Hermes!"[106] Comment on such facets of Heracles' complex personality as gluttony and the like may be postponed until later; here only deception and thievery are under consideration.

Adroitness in deception in the performance of his tasks certainly is not characteristic of him in Pindar at least; his methods are rather those of physical force— wrestling, or use of the club. He is "fearless," "all-daring," possessed from infancy of "extraordinary courage and might." His deeds against "lawless creatures on sea and land" make him approach the culture-hero type of benefactor,[107] and Pindar's attitude to him in the Odes is consistently one of admiration and praise. But, though a passing reference to the theft of the cattle of Geryon in *Isth.* I. 13 contains no condemnation, *Fragment* 169 deals with the same Labor in a critical spirit. *Nomos* (law? rules? custom?) according to this fragment, is the king of all, of both gods and men, and it sometimes compels deeds of the utmost violence—for example, the hero's seizure of the cattle of Geryon "without price or permission." This fragment, quoted widely by Herodotus, Plato, and Aristides, cannot be fairly judged because of lack of context, but it is clear that Pindar had in mind the moral aspect of such seizures. *Fragment* 81 (*Dith.* II) again indicates condemnation: "When I match you with him,/ Geryon, I praise you. But on what Zeus favours not/ I keep silence utterly." The passages have been variously evaluated by scholars. Bowra declares that if the matter concerned "purely human standards, Pindar would take the side of the wronged Geryon against the wrongdoer Heracles, but he recognizes that for the gods [and Heracles is very close to the gods] the matter is different, and therefore he must say nothing about it. The gods follow one set of rules, and men another."[108] To Farnell *Fragment* 169 indicates that Pindar was troubled by the legend; he points out that in several places (the punishment of Coronis' innocent countrymen, and the fate of the sons of Oedipus) the poet remains "on the lower popular level," though he can rise on occasion to a higher conception of the justice of Zeus. A recently discovered fragment of papyrus (*Ox. Pap.* 2450) by a repetition of lines clearly shows that it is a continuation of *Fragment* 169, and Martin Ostwald takes up again the whole question of interpretation. In this continuation a similar seizure of Diomede's horses by Heracles is treated, Diomede is praised for resisting him, and there may be a third criticism of Heracles with regard to the murder of his children by Megara. That the whole tenor of the dithyramb is one condemning Heracles, Ostwald does not believe; somehow or other the poet seeks a means of justifying the acts of Heracles and arrives, though with reluctance, at a conception of *nomos* as "traditional acceptance." He accepts the deeds of Heracles as just when he sees that *nomos,* the traditional attitude which rules over mortals and immortals, makes them so.[109]

The Indians' own attitude to their favorite Trickster ("that ubiquitous scapegrace and culture hero")[110] was also ambivalent. Coffin remarks in the Introduction to his *Indian Tales of North America* that "many modern Indians, confused by this dual role of the trickster, separate a character like Coyote in his good tales from the Coyote of the bad tales."[111] Boas points out that where trickster and culture-hero appear as one person "the benefactions bestowed by the culture-hero are not given in an altruistic spirit, but . . . are means by which he supplies his own needs." On the other hand "the culture-hero of the Pacific coast gives man his arts, and is called 'the one who sets things right.' He is not a trickster, but all his actions have a distinct bearing upon the establishment of the modern order."[112] Such a dichotomy may help to illustrate the differing conceptions of Heracles and Pindar's trouble about them.[113]

42

WINNING A BRIDE

The motif of winning a bride does not of necessity appear among hero-tale motifs, and when it does appear, it often takes the form of a suitor test. The reward must be won by the hero's efforts, and the emphasis is on the accomplishment of the tasks rather than on the romantic interest. There are many of these Suitor Tests or Son-in-Law Tests among the Indian tales we have been considering, the envy or jealousy of the father or his reluctance to bestow his daughter furnishing the motivation. Thompson states that there are thirty such stories in the collection by Boas from Tsimshian mythology. He also refers to an extremely popular story of the North American Indians known as Dirty Boy, in which there is to be a contest for the hand of the chief's daughter. In the various forms of this story the contests are often those of shooting an eagle or of trapping. The hero, often a supernatural being in disguise, may actually win but be cheated by an imposter, though later he assumes his own form and marries the girl. The so-called Son-in-Law Tests are similar to this in theme. Again, in the Swan-Maiden sequence, the hero, who has lost his supernatural wife, comes back from a long search only to find her about to marry another. This, of course, is the famous Penelope motif. He regains her by winning in a contest somewhat as Odysseus wins the Trial of the Bow.[114]

In main motif this tale and the tale of Dirty Boy show a close parallel to Pelops' contest for the hand of Hippodameia in Pindar's first *Olympian*.[115] All the trappings of folklore are here: it was to be a chariot race with the girl's father—a fairly common motif—and (another common motif) death was to be the penalty for defeat. In Pindar's story thirteen of the girl's lovers have met their death, and Pelops prays to the god Poseidon for aid. In one of the poet's "gorgeous epiphanies" the god appears to the youth as he prays by the sea, and gives him winged horses to enable him to outstrip the cruel king. This myth was admirably suited to the ode in which it appears, not only because the myth of Pelops had such close connections with Olympia (Oenomaus was King of Elis, and the famous race later formed the subject for one of the pediments of the temple of Zeus at Olympia), but also because Hiero's victory, which it celebrates, was a victory in the horse race. The ninth *Pythian* treats two other such contests for brides, and again the contests, foot races, are appropriately chosen. The contest which Antaeus of Irasa proposed for the suitors of his daughter is the chief of these. In his dilemma of choosing between them he recalled how Danaus of Argos found husbands for his forty-eight daughters by demanding that they compete in the lists.[116] Greek myths of the winning of a bride usually take the form of such athletic contests, witness the stories of Heracles and Dejanira, Idas and Marpessa, Admetus and Alcestis, Atalanta and Hippomenes. In other folktales, often of literary origin, brides may be won by the hero's cleverness in guessing riddles, by magic, even by making a princess laugh, and in most of these the romantic interest is subordinated to the interest in the contest of wits displayed.

A slightly different turn to the theme is given in one version of the Peleus-Thetis story which appears in *Nemeans* IV and III. This story again has all the marks of a primitive folktale: Peleus wrestles with the Nereid to win her, while she, after the manner of sea-creatures, changes form to lion, dragon, and fire to escape. By sheer endurance, and not by magic means, he holds on until she assumes her rightful shape.[117] A precise classification of this motif does not appear in the *Motif-Index*, though it has similarities with several: Swan motif, Animal Bride, Magical Conflict, Transformation Flight. The last is perhaps the closest, though Transformation to Escape a Lover would be more exact (compare the opposite—Transformation to Seduce). This story of the transformations of Thetis (like the change of her sister Psamathe to a seal to escape Aeacus) seems on a more rational level than the well-known tales of Zeus changing shape to win Leda or Europa, since the nymphs belonged to a race of sea-creatures like Nereus and Proteus, who easily shift form in their fluid environment.

A striking parallel in modern Greek folklore (no doubt a genuine survival of the ancient tale) is recorded from Messenia by J. C. Lawson in his *Modern Greek Folklore and Ancient Greek Religion*. In this tale a young shepherd, who played the pipes for a dance of Nymphs (Nereids), fell in love with one, and was advised by an old woman to seize her kerchief and hold her fast even if she should turn into terrible shapes. He did so and finally won her, though she changed under his grasp into lion, snake, and fire. Frazer, in his edition of Apollodorus, tells a similar tale from Crete.[118]

But another form of the Thetis story is indicated in the eighth *Isthmian*.[119] It is apparently later than the "wrestling" version, and seems an attempt to lift the hero from primitive folktale status to that of a more heroic figure. Because of his exceptional virtue in rebuffing Queen Hippolyte's advances, he is to be rewarded by the gods with a sea-goddess as a bride, thus solving the dilemma of the two gods who were in love with her, yet who had been warned that her son would prove greater than his father. Though this last warning is quite in the spirit of folktale (witness the similar warning to Uranus, who forthwith swallowed his children), the "action of Zeus in regard to Thetis," in the words of Farnell, "is on a much nobler plane than the Hesiodic" version.[120] The gods, taking the advice of Themis, pledged Thetis to Peleus, and attended the wedding in Chiron's cave. The wonderful gifts they brought were later added to the story, and at this wedding the Apple of Discord was thrown, precipitating the Trojan War.

In Greek tales, which seldom stress the purely romantic, the winning of a bride is often only a secondary result of a feat or encounter,[121] the daughter of the taskmaster helping the hero with his task and then eloping with him. This again is a common folktale motif. So Ariadne helps Theseus in his struggle with the Minotaur by giving him the clue, and so, in Pindar's fourth *Pythian*, Medea gives Jason a charm against the breath of the fiery-nostriled bulls and the threat of the dragon guarding the fleece. After telling of this victory, Pindar hurries on, touching only the peaks of the narrative—Medea's flight with Jason and the revenge she took on Pelias[122]—and omitting other motifs associated with the theme such as the scattering of magic objects to delay pursuit, and the hero's desertion of his helper later. A close parallel may be drawn with one of the Indian tales in which the young wife of the hero helps him to meet her father's treachery by giving him magic tobacco to protect him from poisonous snakes, and by warning him that the old man has poisonous lizards in his hair instead of lice.[123]

46

With the frequent animal-marriage themes of Indian tales, Pindar's narratives have nothing to do, unless the "wrestling" version of the Peleus-Thetis story may be considered distantly related.[124]

END OF TALE AND DEATH OF HERO

In the Indian tales the narrative is often brought to an end with the revenge taken on the adversary. An unnatural uncle is dropped from a great height by his persecuted nephew who has assumed the form of an eagle; captured animals avenge themselves, often cruelly, on the person who sends the hero to capture them; or at the end of a contest in magic a boy sets fire to the country and burns up his hostile father.[125] In Pindar, too, though trickery and cruelty are generally condemned, revenge is considered normal and legitimate, and the deaths of the taskmasters are referred to as matter-of-fact acts of justice. "The doer must suffer," as the poet says (*Nemean* IV. 32), quoting a primitive principle of justice attributed to Rhadamanthus by Aristotle. Lawless Pelias and haughty Augeas meet their fates; Polydectes is made to regret with anguish the bride-gift he demanded; the brazen spear of Oenomaus is stayed, and Eurystheus' head is shorn off.[126] Even the revenge taken by Orestes on his mother is seconded by Ares: no Furies follow him, and this at a time when the great trilogy of Aeschylus was presenting so forcefully the evolution of primitive ideas of vengeance toward higher conceptions of justice.[127] In these instances, certainly, Pindar's ideas remain "on the lower popular level," to borrow Farnell's phrase when he is commenting on the fate of the townspeople of Coronis and the fate-driven descendants of Oedipus.[128]

47

A full account of the hero tale would not be complete without some treatment of the death of the hero. Most of the great hero tales come to an end in violence and tragedy, more suited to their protagonists than an old age pitiful with disease or helplessness would be. Since the hero is no ordinary man, ordinary circumstances cannot defeat him, and his death must be brought about by untoward events or treachery of some kind—a poisoned robe for Heracles, a pit of stakes for Rustam, the arrow of an unseen god for Achilles, betrayal or help that comes too late for Theseus, Beowulf, and Roland. The hero often dies young, and pathos is thus added to the tragic ingredients.

In the Indian tales, the death motif seldom occurs: the purpose of these tales, particularly the Trickster ones, is light entertainment, and the hero, often anonymous, is thought of in terms of continued adventures. More serious treatment, however, is given to the culture heroes. They often depart to the West after accomplishing their beneficent deeds, though the sadness of this departure is lightened by the thought of their promised return.[129] So, to use a famous example, Hiawatha (Manabozho) departs in his canoe "in the glory of the sunset" to the Land of the Hereafter.

Pindar, with his fondness for the marvelous and the splendid, at the end of his heroes' mortal life dwells on their glorious future. Heracles is made a god, and his bliss with his divine bride Hebe is acclaimed again and again. Athena confers immortality on her favorite, Diomede (a story that appears first in Pindar); Castor shares the hospitality of Olympus with his brother Polydeuces; Cadmus and Peleus dwell in the Islands of the Blest. Achilles is there, too, or else enjoys immortality in the

White Island.[130] In these Odes, which throughout breathe success and triumph, the painful circumstances of death are omitted altogether or glossed over; we need not be surprised that, although Heracles is treated with far more detail than any other hero, the poisoned robe and flaming death on Oeta do not appear. Tragic endurance in the face of pain and the grim heroic facing of inexorable death and extinction have no place in Pindar's prevailingly optimistic world, unlike the "tragic humanism" which Whitman thinks is the chief virtue of Sophocles' heroes.[131]

There are omissions, natural enough to the glancing lyrical treatment, but in three instances the heroes' death is treated in considerable detail for the purpose of moral reproof. The three, Neoptolemus, Bellerophon, and Ajax, are handled differently. Criticism of Neoptolemus' cruelty at Troy and his god-sent ignominious death at Delphi in *Paean* VI is softened somewhat to a more charitable view in *Nemean* VII. The arrogance of Bellerophon, who attempted to fly to heaven, draws a stern moral from the poet who shrinks with distaste from dwelling on it; the suicide of Ajax, though not entirely condoned, is treated three times with great compassion.[132]

Why the theme of the Return—one of the most striking and admirable features of the Indian tales—does not appear as a formal motif in Greek mythology, is a matter for speculation. The most obvious answer is that it was not needed. The cult of the heroized dead, treated so exhaustively by Farnell, amply compensated for such lack. Heracles and the Dioscuri were customarily worshipped as protectors of the home.[133] Myths of the veneration of the bones of Theseus and Orestes attest the reality of these beliefs, as does the famous story of the appearance of the ghost of Theseus at the battle of Marathon. We are constantly aware in reading the Odes of Pindar that the poet felt vividly the presence of the heroic dead, not only at the great Games where they were at hand to give aid and inspiration, but also at his very side while he thought and wrote. Heracles is personally invoked; Castor and Polydeuces are ever at hand; and even the nymph Aegina, the mother of the famous race of the Aeacids, is once addressed as if actually present.[134] As for the gods themselves, their constant presence was, in Bowra's opinion,[135] more vivid to Pindar than to many of his contemporaries.

DESCRIPTION AND CHARACTERIZATION

One does not expect more than a minimum of description or characterization in oral tales. The persons in them are stock characters, often anonymous; the traits they display concern the events of the story only, and no attempt is made to picture their life outside. Little detailed description is given of them; even in the case of Dirty Boy of the Indian tale, where some realism of description would seem appropriate, few particulars are given. The heroes of the Trickster cycles, too, who might seem distinctive in their cleverness or boastfulness, are, in Boas's words, so "impersonal that they do not represent any individual, but are merely the personifications of greed, amorousness, or silly ambition."[136] In every cultural area, Radin states, "certain animals or beings have become associated with certain definite characteristics," and there are stereotypes for the fool, the humorist, the sloven, the fop, the gossip, which are "supplied from the stock-in-trade of the particular tribe."[137] Greenway

gives a long list, expanded from one of William Rose
Benét, of animals and birds and their associated "characters," pointing out the almost universal agreement on
such traits, though culture, he admits, may have much
to do with certain "aberrant animal symbols." The
Bedouin culture, for example, sees the camel, hideous
beast, as "the paragon of beauty."[138]

There are, however, two rather distinct types of hero
in the American Indian tales, which have been termed
"Dreadnaught" and "Male Cinderella" by their collec-
tors. We have seen a good example of the Dreadnaught
type in the Zuni tale of the two Ahaiyute, the Monster
Slayers: the heroes, in spite of repeated warnings, go at
once to the place of danger, and seemingly never learn
caution from their experiences. On the other hand,
Katherine Spencer describes the heroes of most of the
Navaho Chantway myths as of the "unpromising male
Cinderella" type. The picture, she says, is "of a passive
suffering hero, who is drawn into punishments, ordeals,
trials, and contests, rather than an active conqueror who
undertakes feats of strength, a prolonged quest for a
high goal, or subjection of rivals by cleverness and
wits."[139] Paul Radin even traces development of character in the Winnebago Trickster Cycle he has studied.
Trickster, he thinks, at first an irrational and non-social-
ized being, the prey of all his capricious appetites, finally
returns to his family and to normal living, though
Greenway questions the rigidity of sequence in the
episodes that such a development would presuppose.
Greenway himself believes that Trickster evolves only
in the course of time "into a Culture Hero who con-
sciously performs altruistic acts for man."[140]

In Pindar's glancing lyrical treatment there is little

chance for comparisons here. Animal characters of course do not appear, and much greater sophistication in handling the heroic material is at once evident. In general it may be said that the Greek poet's protagonists carry about them the aura of Homeric heroes, the constant striving for excellence in all things. As Jaeger puts it, "The heroic spirit and the praise of heroism which were the inspiration of the epic are reborn [in Pindar] in lyric form." So Heracles' prayer for the baby Ajax in the presence of his father Telamon seems a reminiscence of Peleus' advice to his son Achilles, and of Hippolochus' for Bellerophon in the Iliad.[141]

We have seen, however, in the treatment of Heracles, Bellerophon, Neoptolemus, and perhaps of Ajax, that Pindar does not always exempt his heroes from criticism. He condemns Peleus and Telamon for the murder of their half-brother Phocus, though he alludes to this crime only indirectly in one of the passages amusingly termed "hush passages," as he self-consciously enjoins silence upon himself in treating an unworthy theme. "Silence is often the wisest thing for a man to observe," he concludes, in speaking of the exile of the brothers from Aegina.[142] Apart from this one criticism of Peleus, the hero is treated as blameless—the man who, in the words of Themis (*Isth.* VIII. 40), was the most pious of all the dwellers in Iolcus, and so most worthy of gaining the sea-goddess Thetis as a bride.

Of personal description and detailed characterization there is little. We are given a flash of the yellow hair of the boy Achilles, a glimpse of the austerity of Peleus, of the courageous philosophy of Pelops, of sly humor in Chiron. With Ajax, that strong speechless man who "wrestled with death," and with Polydeuces, who utters an anguished prayer as he sees his brother dying, we have, however, sudden revelations of genuine dramatic power.[143] The fourth *Pythian*, with its lengthy tale of the Argonauts, gives much more scope to characterization and description. So the poet pictures Jason with his flowing lustrous locks, in Magnesian garb with the leopard skin over his shoulders, appearing at his ancestral home, a combination of strength and daring and beauty, compared by the awestruck bystanders to Ares, or Apollo, or Tityus, surprisingly gentle as he brandishes his two spears. He speaks with "soothing words" to treacherous Pelias, referring to his twenty years spent with the wise Chiron, without ever having said an unbecoming word, or doing an unworthy deed.[144] It is not a very convincing portrait, but it is the most ambitious Pindar ever attempted. One cannot help thinking it was before the eyes of Apollonius in his later epic.

We have already seen that the treatment of Heracles presents certain difficulties. There are two strains in the portraiture of this hero in Greek literature, one the popular and no doubt earlier view of him—burly and boisterous cattle-stealer, glutton, prodigious lover; the other, the hero bound by a tragic fate to his father Zeus, as Pindar puts it, forced to perform tremendous tasks, yet who finally, after driving out lawless monsters and making the seas safe, won godhood and a divine bride, Hebe.[145] This dichotomy, which persists throughout the Greek period, is shown in the burlesque treatment of comic writers and the moralizing statements of the Stoics and other philosophers. Both aspects appear in Pindar. *Fragment* 168 (a and b) reveals his gluttony as witnessed by the Lapith Coronus—the devouring with much crunching of bones the bodies of two roasted oxen;

53

and *Fragment* 171 may refer to the ruthless slaying of Neleus and his young sons, with the exception of the absent Nestor. Criticism of his stealing of Geryon's cattle has been noted above. Ostwald, in the article there mentioned, seems to add to the accusations by stating that Geryon is not depicted as the terrifying triple-bodied monster of other versions of the legend, and that to his knowledge no other Greek author has ever told the story of Heracles' Labors from the standpoint of the hero's victims. His presumption that the dithyrambs are rather late in the Pindaric corpus suggests that in them one may see a real development of Pindar's thought in regard to this hero, who, throughout the Odes, is treated with all the reverence due to a culture hero, and who, after a life of excessive toil, finally wins godhood. One wonders whether the difference in genres may explain a freer treatment in the dithyrambs. Perhaps, too, a closer analysis of the complex Trickster stories may help in clarifying the various aspects of the legends of Heracles, as has been suggested.[146]

No physical description of Heracles is given apart from the epithets referring to his strength and daring, with one exception—a curious passage in *Isthmian* IV. 52—where he is described as "short in stature." This passage has caused much dispute among the critics, some explaining it on the grounds that Pindar's patron was small and insignificant-looking, or that Heracles was small only in comparison with the giant Antaeus, although Pindar's words seem explicit enough. A more probable explanation is that the poet was following some account in local folklore. Though this need not presuppose a hero of the extreme "unpromising" type

Katherine Spencer describes, the small hero who discomfits a gigantic foe is common in folklore everywhere, witness David, Jack the Giant Killer, and the Valiant Tailor in a Grimm tale. The African Trickster, as Mrs. Feldmann points out, is usually an animal of inferior size and strength but superior cleverness, and the popularity of Anansi the Spider in the tales bears out her statement.[147]

If female characters may intrude into this discussion of the hero tale, we may cite Cyrene, the typical huntress of romantic literature, beautiful, athletic, courageous, of the race of Atalanta or of Vergil's Camilla, who wrestles alone with a huge lion, and in contrast, Coronis, in whose heart there was a divided passion, a suggestion in Pindar's art of an interest in dramatic conflict. But the most striking bit appears in the eleventh *Pythian*, where the poet speculates on the motives of Clytemnestra in killing her husband—revenge for the sacrifice of her daughter, or guilty love for Aegisthus.[148] One is reminded inevitably of the *Agamemnon* of Aeschylus, though here a controversy over relative dates enters in—some critics thinking the ode preceded the drama, others that Pindar was influenced by the treatment of Aeschylus.[149]

Miscellaneous Motifs

Pindar seems fascinated by stories of origins, not only those of the great Games, of the separate cities of his clients, or of the numerous inventions of the Greeks,[1] but also those of the beginnings of things, before the stable reign of the Olympian gods pictured in Homer. We are constantly reminded of Hesiod, his great predecessor in Boeotia, his "master," as Farnell has termed him. One of the earliest of his poems, a Hymn to Thebes, which was famous in antiquity, and which occasioned the rebuke of the poetess Corinna mentioned above, may have dealt in its entirety with the theme of creation. In a fragment of this Hymn which has been preserved he tells of the early marriage of Zeus to Themis and the birth of the Hours from this union, as Hesiod does in his *Theogony,* though he differs from Hesiod in terming this the first marriage of Zeus rather than the second. Perhaps, according to Farnell, he wished to avoid the "savage" tale of the swallowing of Metis, whom Hesiod designates as the first wife. In the fragment under consideration, Themis was brought to Olympus by the Fates in their golden chariot from the springs of Ocean.[2] Here possibly may be an allusion to the theory of the "Oceanic" origin of gods and men—a theory which is advanced by Homer in the *Iliad* (XIV. 201).[3]

Uranus and Gaea, Heaven and Earth, the usual primeval pair of Greek mythology, who appear in the creation stories of many peoples, are presented personalized in the Odes as awestruck witnesses of the miraculous birth of Athene;[4] and their children, the Titans, are mentioned in several passages. The loosing

57

of the Titans by the clemency of Zeus (*Pyth.* IV. 291) may be the first appearance of this detail in Greek literature, though their presence as the chorus in the *Prometheus Unbound* of Aeschylus may imply it.[5] The Titan pair, Cronus and Rhea, appear in a passage of the second *Olympian* describing the Islands of the Blest, he as Chief judge and counsellor, while Themis, on Mt. Olympus, plays an active part in advising the gods to avoid a fateful marriage with Thetis.[6] In all these references to early stories of the gods, few parallels may be drawn from the Indian accounts, for the Greek stories have been systematized much more than the Indian, and the gods arranged in carefully developed genealogies. Sky Father and Earth Mother, however, appear often in the Indian tales, and if one wishes to parallel the possible reference to the primacy of water in Pindar's Themis fragment, many instances of this, too, may be found.[7]

Two details of this interesting fragment have not yet been considered—the "shining road" by which the Fates bring Themis in their golden chariot, and the stairway or ladder *(klimax)* by which apparently she is to mount to Olympus. Is the shining road the rainbow or the Milky Way, as some commentators have thought? It is tempting to compare the ladder with the "sky-ropes" of several Indian tales,[8] and even with the ladder of Jacob's dream with the angels ascending and descending. The motif seems to be unique with Pindar. May it be that both of these motifs are charming fancies of the poet's imagination?

The reference to the birth of Athena at which Uranus and Gaea were present deserves special comment. With this grotesque story of her birth from the head of Zeus, which appears twice in Pindar, we are at once at the actual level of primitive thought. Zeus from his own head produced Athena, according to the *Theogony* of Hesiod, and in the spirited Homeric Hymn she is shown springing fully armed from his head, a detail which may have been developed first by Stesichorus. An archaic vase painting shows her as a tiny figure running down from his brows. Pindar is apparently the first author to mention the splitting of the head for the birth. The poet seems to accept the strange story at its face value as a hallowed tradition—there is no hint that he took it as a "patent allegory"—but he puts on his "grandest manner" in treating it. The golden snow shower and the presence of the two primeval divinities lend to it, as Farnell says, the significance of a great cosmic event.[9]

A striking Zuni emergence myth describes four superimposed worlds, progressively darker as they go down, and tells of the struggles of the helpless people in the pitch blackness of the lowest to come up to father Sun.[10] The series of worlds of Greek mythology comes to mind —Tartarus the lowest, and then Hades, the earth, and finally Heaven above all, though the resemblance goes little farther than this except perhaps in vague ideas of imprisonment and "coming up to the sun." The familiar hierarchical Greek system appears in Pindar: "dread" Tartarus, where, following Hesiod, Typhon is imprisoned; Hades, often called the "home of Persephone" —once, picturesquely, the "dark-walled"—where are the rivers that belch forth endless darkness; and above the earth the golden clouds and peaks of Olympus.[11] Acheron is the stream of Hades oftenest mentioned; it is called a ferry and the phrase "deep-sounding shore" suggests this, though boatman Charon does not appear.

A cave called the Mouth of Hades at Taenarus, where the Argonauts should have stopped on their return voyage, is mentioned in *Pythian* IV. 44.[12]

The phrase "cosmology of worlds" is sometimes applied to the Indian conception of the universe. "About the home world of the tribe [this is from Powell's Introduction to Cushing's *Zuñi Folk Tales*] there is gathered a group of worlds, one above, another below, and four more: one at every cardinal point . . . . All of the animals of the tribes, be they human animals, tree animals, star animals, water animals (that is, bodies of water), or stone animals (that is, mountains, hills, valleys, and rocks), have an appropriate habitation in the zenith world, the nadir world, or in one of the cardinal worlds, and their dwelling in the center world is accounted for by some myth of travel to this world."[13] Details of such Indian worlds are of the slightest; the sky was apparently considered a solid floor, resting on the horizon, not far away from earth (in some stories it is pushed away from the earth to make room for mankind); the distance could be spanned by the growth of a tree or the letting down of a rope, while the piercing or digging of a sky-hole could allow entrance or exit.[14] In the Odes (*Pyth.* X. 27) the phrase "brazen heaven, not to be climbed" seems a reminiscence of similar early Greek conceptions; in Homer the adjectives "brazen" and "iron" are often applied to the word "heaven," and the idea of heaven's resting close on earth goes back to Hesiod's *Theogony* (126). The spirit land, or land of the dead, in most primitive mythologies may be placed vaguely in the west or underground, and usually there is a river or body of water which must be crossed to reach it.[15]

The early struggles of the Greek gods against Ty-

phon, the Titans, and the Giants, only casually referred
to by Homer as belonging to a bygone age, Pindar re-
creates vividly, picturing Typhon, the hundred-headed
monster, as finally crushed beneath the weight of Aetna,
where his groans and fiery breath can still be witnessed;
Atlas, still "wrestling with the sky," though his brother
Titans are freed; and especially the Giants, who finally,
their shining tresses dimmed with dust, fell on the plain
of Phlegra beneath the thunderbolt of Zeus and the
twanging bow of Heracles. A fragment of a poem speaks
of Apollo's struggle with the Python.[16] Other fantastic
early creatures—the hundred-handed monsters and the
Cyclopes—are alluded to in the Fragments; the story that
the Cyclopes had built the walls of Tiryns Pindar plainly
knew, and Snell prints tentatively as Fragment 266 a
reference from Philodemus that these creatures were
slain by Zeus because he feared they might provide arms
for one of the gods.[17] All such early enemies of the gods
are usually considered to be nature powers of some sort,
and have their analogues in the storm winds and hostile
monsters of Indian mythology. Frazer, in his edition
of Apollodorus, Appendix II, "The War of Earth on
Heaven," refers to many Indian tales with such themes.[18]

Though Pindar takes much from Hesiod in his description of Typhon, he is unique in mentioning Cilicia
as his home. The resemblance of this fantastic creature
to the Babylonian Tiamat has often been observed, his
Eastern origin almost certain.[19] He was a spectacular
figure to introduce in odes written for victors from
Sicily, where the mythological material was thin, and
Pindar makes much out of his burial beneath Aetna in
his grand description of the volcanic eruption (perhaps
the one about 475 B.C.) caused by his writhings—a de-

scription influencing or influenced by a similar account in the *Prometheus Bound* of Aeschylus.[20] A grotesque tale, quite in keeping with this "savage" myth, that the gods, in terror of Typhon, changed their forms to animals and fled to Egypt, Pindar may also have told, but only to reject it, since it would have offended his ideal of divine dignity.[21]

Besides such tales of the early struggles of the gods we are given a picture of their apportioning the earth in the solemn presence of the Fate, Lachesis, and the island of Rhodes rising from the sea to be the special possession of Helios. The eagles of Zeus fly from the east and west to determine the omphalos of the earth at Delphi, and in the west Heracles sets up the two pillars to be the limit of man's adventurous wanderings.[22] The island of Delos is made fast by four pillars, and Atlas holds up the sky. The idea of four world columns has parallels in other mythologies, as does the conception of the support of the sky on a man's shoulders.[23] The Tsimshian tale, "Strong Man Holds up the Sky," tells of a hero brought by his supernatural helper to an opening in the ground with a long ladder in it which reached down to a platform. Here a very old man with a hemlock pole between his legs was holding up the sky. He had been doing this since the world was made and was very weary. The hero, who had been conditioned by secret rigorous training to feats of physical endurance, and above all to loneliness, cautiously effects the transfer of the pole to his own care, and so releases the old man. If, in his comparison of Damophilus with Atlas (*Pyth.* IV. 289-90), Pindar is thinking of Atlas' banishment and isolation as part of his punishment, there is an interesting parallel to the Tsimshian tale.

Explanations of features of the earth's surface such as springs, mountains, cliffs, and the like, attributed to some god or primitive Paul Bunyan, are frequent enough everywhere to need little particular comment. Thompson says of the North American Indian tales: "Many myths of all the different areas explain physical features of the country. The most usual form of explanation is either that the culture hero deliberately transformed persons into the present physical features or that the many conflicts with the early monsters resulted in changing the face of the country." So Old Man makes the Teton River, and the markings on the rocks near Sault Ste. Marie were left by Manabozho.[24] A definitive study of the explanatory element in American Indian tales was made in 1914 by T. T. Waterman, with a survey of twenty-six mythologies.[25] In these groups of tales instances of explanation of animal traits and topographical features were extremely common, those of heavenly bodies and cosmic forces much fewer than one would expect. As examples of animal and star myths we may read how Raven is blackened by the smoke from the firebrand when he stole fire, and how the Pleiades, fugitives from persecution of some sort, often young girls, rise up and become stars.[26] Childish "Just-So" stories one would not expect to find in sophisticated Greek literature, though Pindar apparently skirts a Hesiodic example explaining the color of the crow in his story of Coronis, and he must have had in mind the Boeotian tale of Orion's pursuit of the mountain nymphs, the Pleiades, in *Nemean* II. 10-12.[27] He speaks, too, of the Muses sending up the spring of Dirce at Thebes,[28] and explains how the olive came to be the victor's crown at Olympia. The myth of the River

Alpheus' pursuit of Arethusa lies beneath his reference to the "breathing-place" of Alpheus in his invocation of Ortygia, Sicily, in the first line of *Nemean* I, just as the story of Poseidon's splitting the Vale of Tempe is implied once in the god's epithet, "Petraios."[29]

But in the article mentioned above, Waterman stressed the point that before such stories could properly be classed as aetiological, the explanatory feature should constitute the main motif and not be incidental or merely tacked on at the end. Greenway, in *Literature among the Primitives,* gives an amusing illustration of such overemphasis: the extraction of minor motifs from complex primitive stories, he says, "is like calling *Moby-Dick 'How Captain Ahab Lost His Leg.'* "[30] Pindar was too much of a poet to let the didactic and explanatory intrude, and in spite of his undoubted interest in origins, it is a far cry from his allusive treatment of myth to the sensational use of explanatory features such as may be seen in the *Metamorphoses* of Ovid. A few other examples of explanatory myths in Pindar will be shown later.[31]

Many of the tales mentioned above testify to the importance of Pindar as a source of mythological information. There were, no doubt, plenty of local "giant myths" that developed in various localities, especially those where there were traces of volcanic activity, but Pindar is our earliest source for a definite myth of the battle of the gods and giants, and the first to moralize this tale. The scholiasts say there was no earlier account of the emergence of the island of Rhodes, and speak of local tales the poet may have heard there. Similarly with regard to Delos—a fragment of the beautiful hymn to the island tells of its having been floating until the arrival of Leto, when the four lofty columns arose on their "adamantine bases." The setting up of the famous Pillars by Heracles is the first mention of this feat in surviving Greek literature, and Strabo speaks of the poet's telling in a lost work of the eagles sent out by Zeus from the East and West to establish Earth's center at Delphi.[32]

Richmond Lattimore comments on this interest of Pindar in myths of origin in a discussion of the *Prometheus Bound* of Aeschylus: "We are asked to imagine an age which . . . is not only pre-heroic and pre-human, but pre-natural. The future of man, the world, the gods, the very laws of nature, are still pendant in process; they have not yet been determined. Only Pindar and Aeschylus, and perhaps Hesiod, could fully project such an age and world."[33]

The creation of man is also the poet's concern. That Pindar knew the commonly accepted theory of the emergence of the first men from the earth is apparent, though there is no reference to Pelasgus, the autochthonous ancestor of the Greeks, in his surviving works. There is, however, a fragment referring to the earth-born origin of Erichthonius, and the name of Erechtheus, an ancestor of the Athenians, an "earth-born" hero, appears in the Odes.[34] But the re-creation of men after the disaster of the Flood is given a prominent place in the ninth *Olympian,* where Deucalion and Pyrrha come down from Mount Parnassus to throw over their shoulders the stones which are to become the second race of men. "Men arose from stones and were called people," a quotation by the scholiast (70a, b) from some unknown epic poet, is the earliest evidence for the tale which probably arose from a popular etymology (*laoi,*

65

people—*laes,* stones), and Pindar may have drawn from this source or from Hesiod, who apparently had treated it too. It is the most striking example in Pindar of the aetiological myth, an explanation, in Halliday's words, "of how, after some cataclysm the present race of men in some particular district were created."[35] That the etymology is false reflects merely on the linguistic ignorance of the time and does not affect the classification of the story. Pindar takes pleasure in the ancient tale, but does not draw from it the symbolism of our descent "from a hard race" as Ovid does in the well-known passage of the *Metamorphoses.*[36]

In Indian myths man is often created from clay, from sticks, feathers, grass, or ears of corn.[37] The Greek story of Prometheus creating man from clay is rather late in origin.[38] It does not appear in Pindar, but there might be evidence that he knew the Orphic theory of man's origin from the ashes of the Titans.[39] The favorite tale of the Thebans was that the Sparti, or Sown-Men from the teeth of the dragon Cadmus slew, were their ancestors. Cadmus appears many times in the Odes, and was given a place of honor in Pindar's description of the Islands of the Blessed. It is evident he knew the story of the Sown-Men from his use of the term *Sparti,* and he may well have told the tale in one of his Odes to the Thebans.[40] The springing of men from teeth has few parallels in folk literature, though it is clearly of folk origin. The doublet myth, Jason's sowing the teeth of the dragon in Aeëtes' field, Pindar in his rapid treatment omits, though he doubtless had it in mind. Farnell gives the most satisfactory reason for the omission: "It is likely he omitted it deliberately, refusing to sanction

66

its transplanting to Kolchis, for at Thebes it was a real ancestor-story."[41]

A few other explanatory myths of origin might be added here. The magic wryneck in the story of the Argonauts (*Pyth.* IV. 213-217) was a special gift of Aphrodite to enable Jason to win Medea, and Pindar tells in *Pythian* XII. 7-11 how the hissing of the snakes on Medusa's head when Perseus decapitated her inspired Athena to an invention. "The purpose of the myth is then apparent," explains Burton. "The poet desires to give a 'Just-So' explanation for the name of a famous piece for the flute," the Many-Headed Tune.[42] The Ritualists may derive some comfort from Pindar's reference to the altar to Athena, Goddess of Horses, which Bellerophon was to raise in gratitude for the gift of the magic bridle (*Ol.* XIII. 82), but who is to say that the myth did not precede the ritual here, as it does in the narrative? To quote Halliday, though not on this passage: "For myth and ritual interact, and if ritual gives rise to myth, myth in turn can give rise to ritual."[43] Pindar's account of the institution of the fireless sacrifices by the Rhodians is not entirely clear. Farnell seems to give the best explanation—that the Rhodians were so intent on watching for the birth of Athena in order to win her favor with the first sacrifice, that they forgot to take fire with them to the citadel. No specific myths accompany the mention of the founding of the various great Games. It seems strange that the picturesque story of the infant Archemorus and the founding of the Nemean Games does not appear.[44]

A treatment of the familiar Olympian gods in Pindar cannot be completed in brief compass; there is no ode in which one or more of them do not appear, and the references are multitudinous. Their aid to heroes, gifts of winged steeds and magic charms, the conferring of immortality on their favorites, as well as their frequent love-affairs with mortal women, have already been mentioned. Zeus, Poseidon, and Apollo appear most frequently, but others of the Olympians are briefly shown: Athena's interest in Perseus and Bellerophon we have just seen; Hera, though hostile to Heracles, lends her aids to the Argonauts; Hermes bears the baby Aristaeus to the Hours for the boon of nectar and ambrosia; Aphrodite welcomes Cyrene to Africa; and Artemis greets Heracles in the land of the Hyperboreans.[45] Self-transformation, that constant resource of the Indian hero, these gods of course may employ—Zeus may appear as Amphitryon or a shower of gold, Triton as Eurypylus —but these deceptions are benevolent in intent, with rational purpose behind them. A spirited and unusual representation of a group of gods at a celebration on Olympus honoring Dionysus and Cybele is given in *Dithyramb* II, the Bacchic frenzy well suggested in excited lines, with wild beasts dancing, the clashing of cymbals, and brandishing of Zeus' thunderbolt. On the whole, they are traditionally represented—Artemis as the virgin huntress, Ares as the bronze-clad warrior, Zeus driving his thunder-car, Apollo and Athena as supreme in dignity and wisdom. They often act as characters in their own right and in their own interests: Apollo strides through the flames of Coronis' funeral pyre to rescue his unborn child; they debate the apportionment of the earth, or the wisdom of a marriage, or the fall of Troy.[46] Lattimore makes an interesting comment on the treatment of gods as dramatic characters in Greek tragedy: "Neither in *Prometheus Bound* nor *The Suppliant*

Maidens, nor anywhere else that I know of in Greek tragedy does Zeus appear in person; other major divinities appear before the audience, but Zeus never."[47] Yet Pindar in the story of Castor and Polydeuces (*Nem.* X) has Zeus make a striking and dramatic appearance, when he speaks to Polydeuces, giving him the choice of forfeiting half his immortality in favor of his dying brother.

Another characteristic of Pindar's treatment of early mythological times is his representation of a close relationship between gods and men, not so much in epiphanies or erotic adventures, as in exchange of hospitality on almost equal terms. This is shown strikingly in the stories of Tantalus, Pelops, and Ixion, as well as in the story of Asclepius, where the powers of a skilled mortal almost equal that of his divine parent. Lattimore comments on such close relationships in his discussion of tragedy referred to above.[48] Some similarity, slight as it is, may be seen in the Indian world, though here one cannot speak readily of gods, but rather of cosmic forces —Sun, Moon, Thunder, South Wind, and the like. In the Blackfoot tale, "The Theft from the Sun," Old Man comes to the Sun's lodge, and the Sun asks him to stay awhile. He does so, is fascinated by the Sun's hunting leggings, which can burn the brush and flush out game, and decides to steal them. The Sun detects the theft and freely gives him the leggings, which later prove a dangerous gift he is glad to be rid of. So Star husbands, in the stories in which they appear, are largely undifferentiated from mortals. A closer approximation to the Greek may be seen in the beautiful Navaho tale of Dawn Boy, who went on a rainbow up rocky cliffs to the White House, where the Talking God and the House God challenged his entrance. "Who is this stranger that

69

enters our house unbidden? Is he one of the People on Earth?" Dawn Boy shows them the precious stones and shells he has brought with him as gifts, they are appeased, tell him he is welcome to remain, and in return teach him songs and the White House prayer.[49] With this interchange of gifts one's thoughts may return to Pindar and his account of the blissful weddings of Peleus and Cadmus to divinities, when the Muses sang, and the gods brought gifts to the happy couples:

> "Yet men say these two were given
> blessedness beyond all mortals. They hear on the
>   mountain
> and at seven-gated Thebes the gold-chapleted
>   Muses singing
> when one married ox-eyed Harmonia and the other
> wise Nereus' legendary daughter, Thetis.
>
> "And the gods feasted beside them each in turn,
> and they saw the kings, the sons of Kronos, in their
>   golden chairs, and accepted
> their gifts."[50] (*Pyth.* III. 88-95, translated by
>   Richmond Lattimore.)

After Pindar greater sophistication comes in, and the gulf between heaven and earth widens. There is no longer depicted this early "close and cordial" relationship between gods and men.

TABU

A primitive theme, that of tabu, treated by Thompson as an entire chapter in his *Motif-Index,* is common in the Indian tales, though it often appears, not in the form of compulsive ceremonial rules of avoidance, but merely as good-natured warnings given the characters by relatives or friends. These serve chiefly to increase the narrative tension. An amusing example occurs in the Zuni tale, "The Monster Slayers," in which the two heroes, the Ahaiyute, are cautioned repeatedly by their grandmother not to go toward the East, the South, the Southwest, the North. "All right!" they cheerfully assent each time, but each time immediately disobey, to meet, of course, the penalties of disobedience. For the Sky World and the Land of the Dead the tabus are more emphatically and specifically defined. The Girl Enticed to the Sky is forbidden by her husband to dig deep for herbs and roots; she does so and uncovers a window in the sky through which she attempts to escape. But the rope of sinew she has secretly made is not long enough to reach the earth, and she dangles helplessly until her husband relents and releases her. Those who visit the Land of the Dead must not speak to the spirits or touch them or even look at them, and if they attempt to bring them back to earth the tabus are stricter still. The related idea of the danger of encroaching on the domain of the gods lies beneath the story of the Man Who Acted as the Sun—a striking parallel to the Greek story of Phaethon, and one ending in a similar disastrous conflagration.[51]

The tabus which are latent in Pindar's tales, too, have to do chiefly with infringements on the province of the gods. *Hybris* was a favorite word with the Greek moralists, and "Mortal thoughts befit men" (*Isth.* V. 16) was similar to the sayings of the Seven Wise Men inscribed on the temple of Apollo at Delphi. The sin of Tantalus was to steal the forbidden food of the gods; Asclepius, tempted by gold, restored a man to life.[52]

71

Tityus and Ixion both impiously desired the love of goddesses, and Bellerophon tried to mount to heaven on his winged steed.[53] The giants Otus and Ephialtes attempted the ascent in a different way—by piling mountains on each other (*Fr.* 162): "stretching a quick scaling-ladder to reach steep heaven."[54] This Tower of Babel theme has its interesting counterparts in primitive literature elsewhere. An Ashanti tale—"The Tower to Heaven"—relates how an old woman, wanting to reach Onyankopon, who had left man and taken himself up into the sky, instructed her children to bring all the mortars they could find and pile them on top of each other. They obeyed but found they lacked one to reach Onyankopon. But on her subsequent advice to take one from the bottom and put it on top to make them reach, the whole structure collapsed, causing the death of many people. Another tale from Africa, "The Old Woman Who Tried to Find God," tells of her toiling to build a wooden structure whose lower timbers kept constantly rotting and collapsing.[55] The irony of these futile attempts is not so much stressed in the Greek stories as is man's insolent ambition. "Seek not vainly to become a god" is Pindar's warning again and again. Beneath the phrases "boldly-daring Salmoneus" and "thunderstruck Semele"[56] may lie in the poet's mind other well-known tales of presumptuous encroachment on the domain of the gods: he by imitating Zeus's thunder and lightning, she by looking on the god in all his splendor. Summary punishment or death was the end for all of these except Semele. For her the tabu of looking on a god apparently worked automatically; her death was brought about by no conscious sin, and she was admitted to Olympus and honored there. "If any man strains his eyes for things afar, he is too short to reach the bronze-paved abode of the gods," the poet concludes, in commenting on the fall of Bellerophon. The girl in the Indian story, "Girl Enticed to the Sky," found that her rope for descent was not long enough. Greek and Indian thought, though starting from different points of view, is here the same.[57]

THE DEAD

If the tales in *The Story Telling Stone* form a fair sampling of Indian material, the preoccupation of the Indians with death, especially with attempts to explain how death came into the world, is considerable. The Land of the Dead is imagined usually in the West, often beyond some stream or body of water, and as we have seen, there are several tales of attempted journeys to that land. These tales show great imaginative power, and some of them poignant pathos in the description of futile attempts to bring back spirits to the land of the living. Punishment in the future life does not seem to be a part of the usual Indian conception. There is dancing with much beating of drums for the spirits every night (they sleep during the day), and there is an abundance of food to eat. They seem to have no positive yearning to return to the living.[58]

In the Odes the few references to the house of "dark-walled Persephone" show the conventional picture of the place, as we have seen. Few of the dead are shown there, though they are far from being the witless ghosts Odysseus pitied in his visit in the *Odyssey*. Pindar thinks of them as sentient and as taking pleasure in the report of their descendants' victories when news is brought to them by Angelia, the daughter of Hermes.[59] Coronis goes to the home of Hades as a punishment for her infidelity, and Tantalus is punished with a great boulder hanging over him, constantly threatening to fall. This differs from the account in the *Odyssey,* where he is tortured by both hunger and thirst. The overhanging stone appears first in Archilochus and became proverbial for any constant threatening danger. Pindar (*Isthmian* VIII. 10) may be referring to the Persian invasion as a "stone of Tantalus." But the passage in the first *Olympian* referring to the sinner is obscure, both as regards the place of punishment (Hades? Olympus?) and his "three companions" (Tityus, Sisyphus, the Danaids? or thirst, hunger, immortality?).[60]

The long passage in the second *Olympian* and several fragments of Dirges—all perhaps tinged with Orphic beliefs—give further suggestions of Pindar's views of the future life.[61] Hades here seems to be conceived as a place of two divisions, the just enjoying sunshine, music, and games (much as in the Indian tales), the unjust toiling in utter darkness, both abodes connected with life in this earth by a threefold process of reincarnation. The souls who successfully pass the threefold testing travel by the "highway of Zeus" to the "Tower of Cronus" and the Islands of the Blessed, there to enjoy eternal bliss. Some mystic significance may lie in the Highway and the Tower—the phrases are unique with Pindar—or, as with the "shining path" and "stairway to Heaven" referred to in the Themis fragment above, they may be creations of the poet's fancy.[62] He has lavished all the splendors of his imagination on these abodes of the good, with their crimson roses and golden

74

water-flowers bright in everlasting sunshine, with Rhadamanthus, the kindly judge, enthroned above all in the eternal abode. The heroes who journey there seem to have experienced no death; Achilles was translated there, with the consent of Zeus, by his mother Thetis.[63]

For the heroes who win immortality on Olympus, actual transportation is sometimes offered by the gods themselves. Poseidon with his golden chariot carried off Pelops bodily, as Zeus had borne Ganymede. With regard to the way Heracles, Diomede, and Semele reached heaven we are given no hints, nor of the routes taken by Castor and Polydeuces in their repeated journeys to Hades from Olympus on alternate days. The Hours and Mother Earth were to assure immortality to Cyrene's child Aristaeus by dropping nectar and ambrosia on his lips, according to Chiron's prophecy to Apollo.[64] It seems unfortunate that such conferring of immortality by the gods on mortals should be classified in the *Motif-Index* as mere manifestations of magic power, and that bodily translation should not receive special notice. When Glaucus the fisherman eats the magic grass and becomes a sea-god, we are on the level of magic—far below other deifications in dignity and significance. Actual instances of deification in Greek mythology are selective and few, and such deifications demand exalted powers.

Perhaps some comment should here be made on the reversal of the process—a de-immortalizing, if such a preposterous word may be allowed. For according to Pindar (*Ol.* I. 65-66), "The gods returned Pelops to the quick-fated race of men"—a curious statement and one for which no second example comes readily to mind. Perhaps Tennyson's line, "The gods themselves cannot recall their gifts," repeats itself in one's thoughts too insistently. The *Homeric Hymn to Aphrodite* (218-238), no doubt in Tennyson's mind when he wrote his "Tithonus," certainly implies that Zeus' gift of immortality could not be recalled, though there is no express statement to that effect. Apollodorus, in speaking of the inadvertent wounding of Chiron by Heracles (II. 5. 4), clearly states that the centaur could not die, because he was immortal; he must find a substitute to whom to pass his immortality in exchange for death, much as Polydeuces in Pindar gives up half of his to his dying brother. Pindar, in his anxiety to dispose of the story of the cannibal feast by giving a new explanation of Pelops' temporary disappearance, may have involved himself in a difficulty here. The critics seem of no help, absorbed as they are in other aspects of the Pelops story.[65]

Another kind of translation, called by Rohde "subterranean translation,"[66] appears in several stories of Greek mythology, those of Trophonius and Amphiaraus especially. Both these heroes were close to Theban Pindar; Trophonius had a shrine near Lebadea in Boeotia, and Amphiaraus was famous for his part in the disastrous war of the Seven against Thebes. He is a favorite with Pindar, who tells dramatically the tale of his being swallowed by the earth, chariot and all, when it was cleft by Zeus' thunderbolt; his voice thereafter came from his shrine near by, proclaiming the fate of the second expedition against the city.[67] These "translations" differed from those to the Islands of the Blessed in that they were local, and the divine or semi-divine heroes could be addressed by the living. They apparently were thought of as dwelling in the usual Hades, though in a special accessible place.

But the most curious instance in Pindar is that of Caeneus the invulnerable Lapith. A fragment telling of the famous battle of the Centaurs and Lapiths is preserved by the scholiast on Apollonius of Rhodes' *Argonautica* I. 59-64, which tells how "unconquered and unyielding he passed beneath the earth," buried alive by the pine tree weapons of the Centaurs. Pindar adds the strange detail that he stamped with his foot, cleaving the earth, and so passed beneath it.[68] Here two points bear on folklore material—the motif of the Unique Exception (wood being the one fatal weapon, much like the mistletoe for Balder), and the power of stamping with one's foot to make a passage to the Lower World. Rohde makes much of the fact that he descends *upright*.[69] The *Motif-Index* gives no help in classification here, and parallels are hard to find. Striking the earth with one's hands was a common way of calling on the divinities below to hear; so Meleager's mother in the *Iliad* (IX. 568) invokes curses on her son. In the Indian story, "The Two Sisters," Juka sinks into the ground and Haka Lasi into a lake,[70] but a closer parallel is found in the West Ceram tale of the divine maiden Rabia who sinks into the earth among the roots of a tree, later to appear as the moon. In another myth from the same locality the girl Hainuwele is enticed to the center of the dancing ground, thrown into a hole carefully prepared there, and trampled firmly down by the dancers. Here there is clearly some ritual significance: "the killing or sacrificing of . . . powerful beings effects a redistribution of power. . . . The parts of the sacrificed beings become the stable and life-giving sources of the cosmos."[71] But there seem to be no such ritual connections with Caeneus, who, according to later myth writers, had the power of change of sex granted him by Poseidon, and whose story otherwise displays features of folk belief in that (Ovid is the author here) from under the heap of fir branches the spectators saw a bright-winged bird escape and fly away—presumably the soul of Caeneus.[72] It is strange that Hyginus lists him among the group of suicides he gathers together. A few critics think he may have been some sort of chthonic deity, though there seems to be no evidence for his worship.[73] The riddle of Caeneus is far from being solved; the evidence is too scanty.

We are familiar with the idea of the gods' striking the earth and plunging their enemies into Tartarus from Hesiod's tales of the fate of the Titans and Typhon. In a fragment of a Paean by Pindar,[74] Euxantius of the island of Ceos tells an obscure tale which was no doubt part of the folklore of the island. Zeus and Poseidon, angered perhaps because of the insolence of the inhabitants, plunged the land and its people, all except Euxantius' mother and her home, into the depths of Tartarus—an act curiously reminiscent of early crude acts of vengeance on the part of the gods. Wicked cities or chapels sunk into the sea or into lakes come to mind, though not enough is known about the Euxantius story to make fruitful any close drawing of parallels. Poe's "City in the Sea" is not described expressly as a wicked one, though Death had "reared it as his throne," and when it finally sinks into the sea, Hell itself rises to do it reverence.

Asclepius once, as we have seen, restored the dead to life, but this power generally is the prerogative of the gods. So Zeus, in the usual version of the story of the Dioscuri, revives Castor, though Pindar's reference to the resuscitation in *Nem.* X. 90 is unclear, and he may mean that the immortal brother Polydeuces confers the gift instead.

Resuscitation by the gods of the dismembered body of Pelops, so savagely slain and served to them by Tantalus, was the well-known version of the tale, but Pindar alters it, and has Clotho lift the child Pelops from the birthbath instead, his gleaming ivory shoulder a conspicuous birthmark. He was whisked up to heaven by Poseidon (when the child grew to maturity is not disclosed), and later returned "to the race of men."[75] But a stranger story of resuscitation or of rejuvenescence was told of Iolaus. This loyal nephew of Heracles, according to the scholiast on l. 80 (137a) of the ninth *Pythian,* rose from the dead (or was rejuvenated according to Euripides in *The Children of Heracles,* l. 850) to slay Eurystheus and save Heracles' children. Pindar omits details of the well-known tale, contenting himself with saying he was buried beside the tomb of Amphitryon, "when he had cut off the head of Eurystheus."[76] We are not favored, then, with a picture of his ghostly presence, or with the miracle of the aged man, who, after a prayer to Hebe and to Zeus, regained his youthful strength for a day, as in the drama of Euripides, but some such story is latent beneath Pindar's lines.

A ghost *is* mentioned, though—the ghost of Phrixus, who appeared to King Pelias in a dream and pleaded to be brought back from Colchis, where he had been carried by the golden-fleeced Ram (*Pyth.* IV. 159 ff.). It is true he may not have been a bona fide ghost (his appearance is unique with Pindar), but an invention of the crafty king to justify his sending Jason for the Fleece. But *anaclesis,* the summoning of the dead home if they died in a foreign land, was a well-known practice, and the excuse was legitimate enough. As Farnell says, the detail adds a solemn and religious note to the tale, and perhaps for this reason Pindar inserted it.[77] We are near, in any event, to the folklore motif, the Unquiet Grave. The night oracle of Amphiaraus from his tomb brings us nearer to popular belief in ghostly presences, as do the nightly sacrifices to the children of Heracles described in *Isthmian* IV. 61 ff. These last were probably propitiatory: "Even a child ghost could be vindictive and need atonement," though Pindar may have rejected the idea that Heracles murdered his children.[78]

DECEPTIONS

Pindar seems to have been the first to put into poetic form the story of Ixion, some points of which have already been touched upon. At this time we are concerned with the "cloud Hera" which Zeus fashioned to deceive him, and which led to his punishment on a four-spoked wheel that revolved constantly. Some folklorists have busied themselves with this wheel (a symbol of the sun? an indication of former ritual sacrifices, or of burning disks at fire-festivals?),[79] but it seems simpler and more in keeping with poetic imagination to liken it ironically to the magic iynx, that wheel with the bird, a wryneck, attached, by which estranged lovers were summoned and compelled. Pindar seems strangely impressed by this magic device. He imagines it to have been invented by Aphrodite and given to Jason to secure the love of Medea in Colchis—a detail which is Pindar's own—and he once claims he is drawn by a "magic iynx" that lies on his heart to press on to other themes.[80] The appropriateness of Ixion's instrument of torture to this wheel of passion Finley has pointed out; the description of it as "four-spoked" is similar to that of the magic wheel of Aphrodite.[81] As for the "cloud Hera," Farnell has seen the "true touch of folklore" in the fact that Nephele, far from being a cloud which dissolves at touch, can give birth like a real woman.[82] The scholiast on Apollonius of Rhodes' *Argonautica* (IV. 57) gives what is apparently a doublet myth: "In the *Great Eoiae* [of Hesiod?] it is said that Endymion was carried by Zeus to heaven, but when he fell in love with Hera was deceived with a cloud-shape, and was cast out and went down into Hades." With the thought of such deceptive cloud-shapes the story of Stesichorus' famous palinode comes to mind. The poet, struck blind by what he imagined to be the anger of Helen at his former vilification, sought to appease her by recanting: Helen herself did not go to Troy, but a phantom Helen fashioned of clouds (by Zeus? Aphrodite? Proteus?) deceived both Greeks and Trojans during the long siege.[83] This theme of illusion permeates every part of Euripides' *Helen,* as Lattimore says in his discussion of the play.[84]

But the motif of the Cloud Bride or Phantom Bride has not been fully explored. The *Motif-Index* gives no exact parallel. There was plenty of room for the macabre in Pindar's conception: one thinks of the Indian tales in which a husband brings back his wife from the Land of Spirits believing her to be alive again, but wakes to find himself clutching a corpse or a skeleton.[85] In Catherine H. Berndt's weird story from New Guinea, "The Ghost Husband," the skin fall in a heap from the dead person, here a man, leaving only the bones.[86] Poe's

"Ligeia" illustrates a slightly different treatment of the same theme. But Pindar's cloud wraith appears as a "bane of beauty"; the poet omits Ixion's disillusionment and terror when he realizes the trick, and abhorrence at the unnatural union is expressed, chiefly through the monstrous offspring Centaurus. "A mother unique, a son unique"—Pindar's condensed phrase—is admirably translated by Seymour as "Never such a mother, never such a son." Pindar's addition to the story—the mating of Centaurus with Magnesian mares to produce the race of the Centaurs—brings us at once within the well-known precincts of folklore to stories of animal unions, though Centaurus seems to be an intermediate creature of Pindar's devising. The Centaurs are usually given an entirely different parentage, or else Nephele (Cloud) is their actual mother. Confusion of name and meaning might, of course, give rise to such stories.[87]

Jaeger in his *Paideia*[88] speaks of Pindar as "archaic" and equates him with Hesiod in this respect. "Although Hesiod was a faithful student of Homer and of Ionian ideas," he says, "the reader of Hesiod is often astonished by sudden glimpses into the dark prehistory of mainland Greece, buried far beneath the foundations of the epic. Much more so, when we open Pindar, we are at once in a world unknown to the Ionia of Hecataeus and Heraclitus, a world which is in many ways older than Homer and Homer's characters, lit as they are by the first brilliance of Ionian thought." Pindar does not, for example, shrink entirely from speaking of savage atrocities (as Homer did, according to Gilbert Murray) such as the cruel deception practiced on the gods by Tantalus in serving up to them his son Pelops, and their resulting cannibalism. Bowra says he seems to linger over the gruesome details with relish.[89] Yet his sense of reverence, which led him to reject that story as untrue, probably caused him to avoid details of other stories which doubtless he was aware of, or to mention them only for the sake of rejection. One such is the fragment stating that Hephaestus made for his mother a magic chair from which she was unable to rise.[90] This is clearly a *Märchen* motif. The bewitched saddle on which the Rich Man in the Grimm tale, "Rich Man and Poor Man," foolishly wishes his wife to sit, comes at once to mind. The Greek tale, a popular one, commonly referred to as the Binding of Hera, was represented dramatically on the early François Vase, with Hephaestus brought back on a donkey to rescue his mother when all the efforts of the gods to free her had failed. Farnell excuses the poet's "undignified" story, explaining it as an example of his characteristic coldness toward Hera, who had shown herself hostile to his favorite hero Heracles;[91] Plato in his *Republic* (II. 378 D) rejects the story outright on moral grounds. Pindar's probable rejection of the story of the gods' changing to animal forms to escape Typhon has already been alluded to, and the frequency of such deceptions, often cruel in nature, in the Indian tales has been noted in the first chapter. Self-transformations of the gods, usually benevolent in intent in their dealings with mortals, have also been mentioned, though once Pindar states that Apollo, in anger at Achilles, assumed the form of Paris to aim his swift arrows at that hero and cause his death.[92] Of an ambiguous character is the deception practiced by the same god on Agamedes and Trophonius, builders of his temple at Delphi: When they asked for the pay due them, the god promised to give it on the seventh day; meanwhile they should feast and be merry. But on the seventh night the two died in their sleep—an ironical comment on the good gifts of the gods, if Plutarch recounts the story rightly.[93]

PROPHECY

The section on Ordaining the Future does not occupy a very large place in the Thompson *Motif-Index,* though one motif in it is of considerable importance— that of the poor or unknown child of whose future great things are promised. The relative unimportance of this section is in direct contrast to Pindar's treatment, for of all the themes in the works of the poet this one occurs by far the most frequently. In fact in Greek mythology as a whole one could almost hazard a guess that Prophecy Fulfilled is the favorite theme if one wished to pick out a dominant one. Though seers and prophets enough exist, most characteristic of the Greek treatment is the oracle, especially the one at Delphi, whose prominence in history is reflected in multitudinous myths. The oracle serves two purposes: it provides advice as well as the prediction of future events, and in both of these carries the sanction of divine authority. As a narrative device authors can conveniently use it as a means of unifying their material.

It is this stamp of authority that differentiates the treatment of the theme in Pindar most sharply from that generally found in folktales, where, as Thompson points out, the prophecies are seldom given by rational or intelligent beings, but often by children, old and witless people, dying men, and even by animals.[94] Survivals of such folktale characteristics linger in Homer where prophecies of dying men occur, often in defiance of physiological probabilities. The prophecy of Achilles' horse in the *Iliad* seems a startling throwback to the primitive, though the poet took pains to explain that the goddess Hera expressly gave him speech.[95]

Since Apollo, the god of prophecy, was pre-eminently Pindar's patron god (Pausanias states that the chair of Pindar stood at Delphi, and whenever Pindar came to Delphi he would sit in this chair and sing his songs to Apollo),[96] it is natural that Apollo and his oracle should be most frequently mentioned in the Odes, though of course Zeus, chief of gods, shares the prominence. The Titan goddess Themis and the Fates, too, appear, as well as Chiron, the "divine beast," and a host of major and minor prophets and seers—Tiresias, prophet of Zeus; Tenerus, son of Apollo and the nymph Melia; the Iamidae, descended from Apollo's son Iamus; Polyidus, Melampus, and Mopsus. Pindar seems to have been the first to endow Cassandra with prophetic powers, and in the story of the Argonauts Medea adds this ability to her formidable magic repertoire. Even Heracles, with the help of a favorable omen from Zeus, ventures to foretell the future prowess of Telamon's unborn son, Ajax.[97]

To add to the variety, there is mention of Apollo's Ismenian temple at Thebes, the place of "truthful oracles," the oracle of the dead at the tomb of Amphiaraus, references to pyromancy, interpretation of the flight of birds, omens in the thunder of Zeus, the nods of the gods to confirm a decree, and prophetic dreams and visions.[98]

The motif of the prophecy about the future of a child or yet unborn babe appears several times in Pindar, reminding one of Aarne-Thompson's Tale Type

930, Prophecy of Future Greatness. A conspicuous example is found in *Nemean* I. 61, where Tiresias foretells the heroic achievements of Heracles after the baby has strangled the snakes sent by Hera. Again, in shorter compass, Aepytus tells of the oracle of Apollo which predicted a glorious future for Iamus, child of his daughter by Apollo (*Ol.* VI. 47). Themis, when both Zeus and Poseidon were rivals for the hand of Thetis, dissuaded them by the prediction that Thetis would bear a son "stronger than his father," and Chiron, once, in amusing deference to the great god of prophecy himself, seconded the god's union with Cyrene, and foretold the birth and achievements of their son, Aristaeus (*Pyth.* IX. 59). Heracles' prophecy about the infant Ajax has already been mentioned.[99]

One of the most widespread themes, appearing in both oral and literary tales, is the Oedipus theme, that of the son destined to slay his father and marry his mother. Since this is a Theban story, it is not surprising to find references to it in Pindar, the Theban poet. In *Olympian* II. 38, there is a glancing allusion to it by what we may call the "prophetic flashback"—stating the event before giving the prophecy which foretold the event—a technique made natural by the fact that the story was such a well-known one that no suspense could be generated. It is used by Pindar here to illustrate his philosophical treatment of inevitable changes of fortune. *Fragment* 68 also contains an allusion to a prophecy given to Laius, which the scholiast on *Ol.* II. 39 (70d) explains as a warning not to beget a child. A forecast of one's own death, again a common folktale motif, appears in the oracle given to Pelias about the one-sandaled man, and Pelias, in true folktale style, does his best to avoid fulfilment by sending Jason on a dangerous mission. Amphiaraus' oracle at his tomb foretells the success of Adrastus' second attack on Thebes and of the death of Adrastus' own son (Aegialeus) who alone among Adrastus' army is destined to die in the attack.[100]

A frequent and fundamental function of the Greek oracle was to advise would-be colonists on their plans. Here, naturally, no folktale similarities can be found. The convenience of these oracles to the poet who wished to glorify the ancestors of his athletic patrons is apparent. So, in Pindar, Pyrrha and Deucalion are sent by Zeus to Protogeneia after the Flood (*Ol.* IX. 41), Tlepolemus is told to go to Rhodes (*Ol.* VII. 32), and Battus is sent to Cyrene (*Pyth.* IV. 7, 60 and V. 55). The accomplishment of other tasks also may be predicted: Polyidus gives instructions to Bellerophon for winning the gods' favor (*Ol.* XIII. 74), and Mopsus foretells the success of the Argonauts (*Pyth.* IV. 191).

The ingenuity of the Greeks in explaining the length of the siege of Troy and its final destruction by the necessary fulfillment of various oracles is astonishing. It was the decree of the gods that Troy should fall, as Homer often states. The portent of the snake and the nine birds in the *Iliad* indicated the length of the war; the first person slain would bring victory to his side; the city could not be taken until the arrows of Heracles were brought, until the statue of Pallas was removed, until Neoptolemus was summoned from Scyros; the horses of Rhesus must not drink from the Scamander. On the Trojan side there were prophecies, too: those of Cassandra, and Hecuba's dream that she would give birth to a firebrand. Though some of these appear in late rather than

87

early authors, the length of the list illustrates the persistent Greek preoccupation with prophecy. Pindar uses a fair number of them—the decree of the gods, Hecuba's dream, Cassandra's prophecies, and the prophecy about the arrows of Heracles which must be taken to Troy.[101] He adds still another—one appearing in no other writer, according to the scholiast—the omen of the three snakes attempting to scale the wall of Troy, and Apollo's interpretation of the omen (*Ol.* VIII. 37-46 [41a]). Apollo and Poseidon had asked Aeacus' aid in building the walls; two snakes failed to scale them where the gods had built, but where the mortal Aeacus had helped, the third snake made his entrance. This was the plan of the gods; otherwise the city would have been impregnable. A favorite device in many of these prophecies is making the event (for example, the fall of Troy) contingent on a definite happening—the case of the Unique Exception. Thompson devotes half of his section Z to motifs of this kind. The Greeks seem to have favored it exceedingly—the classic example being Achilles' vulnerability in his heel alone.

A kind of double treatment is given to prophecies about Neoptolemus: according to one, it was fated that the man who slew Priam should never return home; according to another, it was fated that one of the race of the Aeacidae should die at Delphi. The death of Neoptolemus at Delphi made both these prophecies come true.[102]

In the North American Indian tales surveyed there are no prophecies like these just mentioned which span a sizable part of the stories—in fact, no formal predictions at all.[103] Such construction would imply a degree of sophistication in narrative art perhaps too advanced for oral tales. There are several warnings and tabus, as we have seen, which serve a similar purpose, but disobedience and its consequences follow so quickly upon the warning that narrative suspense is not raised. Neither is suspense exploited in Pindar's treatment; few narratives are sustained long enough to allow for it. The longest span between prophecy and fulfillment occurs in *Pythian* IV, where the prophecy of the death of Pelias by a man wearing one sandal is not formally "answered" until the mention of his death several hundred lines later. Indeed the whole treatment of prophecy in this long narrative, seconded by the symbolism of the clod which was to assure Battus' descendants of their future rule in Africa, indicates a complexity of narrative technique far removed from the simple structure of folktales. On the whole, however, one has the feeling that most of these stories were so familiar to the Greek audience that the chief pleasure derived from this favorite device was the satisfaction derived from a neat tying together of ends—a sense of orderliness that appealed strongly to the Greek mind. The cases of "prophecy fulfilled" are mostly used to illustrate the wisdom and omniscience of the gods, or the wonder of mortal happenings.

UNNATURAL CRUELTY

Thompson (*The Folktale,* p. 201) has commented on the prevalence of tales of violence in simple societies everywhere, for such stories, as he says, "come from people used to severe elemental conflicts in their own lives and interested in such conflicts when they hear tales of others." Two passages of Pindar already treated under Deceptions might be mentioned again here, since they both involve unnatural cruelty—the initial crime of Ixion, who was the first man to shed the blood of one of his own relatives, and the story of Tantalus serving his Pelops to the gods. But the Tantalus story Pindar rejects in one of his famous "hush" passages, and he does not give details of the crime of Ixion. Such rejection seems to be a frequent practice. He refrains from speaking of the reason for the exile of Peleus and Telamon—the murder of their half-brother, Phocus. Though he mentions propitiatory sacrifices for the slain children of Heracles, he apparently does not attribute the murder to Heracles, or else keeps silent about it.[104] In a similar way he omits the reasons behind Athena's act in conferring immortality upon Diomede. The scholiast tells the story: Athena had intended her gift for Diomede's father Tydeus, but was revolted by that hero's savage conduct on the battlefield in gulping down the brains of his slain foe, and transferred the favor to Diomede instead. Just so in the *Mahabharata* Bhima drank his enemy's blood. Behind such revolting acts apparently lay the savage belief that by these means one would acquire the dead foe's valor.[105] Elsewhere in Pindar murder is condemned—the "slaughter" of Iphigenia, the murder of Cassandra and Agamemnon by the pitiless Clytemnestra—and also various acts of persecution. The story of the fifty daughters of Danaus, commanded by their father to slay their bridegrooms on the wedding night, Pindar omits, taking it for granted his audience is familiar with it; but he indicates his judgment by praising Hypermnestra, who alone refrained from the act and spared her husband.[106] That revenge for injustice was, however, often considered legitimate, we have already seen.

90

SEX

Stories of the numerous amours of the gods with mortal women, often regarded as the most serious blemish on the highly imaginative mythology of the Greeks, Pindar apparently accepted in good faith, though his contemporary, Xenophanes, bitterly inveighed against them. From such unions rose the heroes he was proud to celebrate, and the mortal women so honored, like Alcmena and Aegina, were thought to cast glory on their native states. Certain parts of these stories, however, which he undoubtedly knew, and which contained crude or irrational elements, he noticeably refrained from mentioning. That he knew the tale of Asteria's leap into the sea to become the island of Delos is apparent from the harsh metaphor, "body of Asteria," he applies to the island in a fragment of a Paean. Farnell explains: "Pindar was aware of the legend that Asteria had rejected the love of Zeus, and as a penalty was cast into the sea and changed into a rock . . . ; but the most probable interpretation of that mutilated text is that Pindar rejected the story as incredible and degrading."[107] For a similar reason he may have omitted the cause of Taygete's transformation into a hind in *Olympian* III (the scholiasts say Artemis came to her aid to help her escape the pursuit of Zeus),[108] and canceled completely all references to the well-known tale of Zeus' abduction of Aegina with the crude feature of the god's self-transformation into a stone to save himself from her angry father. Instead, the happy union of the two is celebrated several times in the Odes.[109] His delight in alluding to the marriages of Peleus and Cadmus to goddesses we have already seen. He may also have told the affecting tale of Rhoecus and the tree-nymph whose messenger was a bee.[110]

Tale Types

This survey so far must have created the impression that the mythical material in Pindar consists chiefly of isolated motifs. Such an impression is not accurate, of course, as a straightforward reading of the Odes would quickly show. There are several narratives which have all the characteristics of complete short stories, showing development of plot, dramatic opposition, climax, and a bit of characterization.[111] Such, for example, are the tales of Coronis and of Ixion, which might be entitled The Unfaithful Wife and the Ungrateful Guest. Folklorists are particularly interested in tracing the ancestry and variants of such tale types, though the two just mentioned would probably not attract their attention, since they are too general in nature and incident to warrant any conclusions as to origin or relationship. As Halliday puts it:[112] "Only stories which substantially repeat the same plot, that is to say the same series of incidents arranged in the same logical order of interest, in which the variation is limited to obvious or accidental omissions or modifications, can fairly be treated as variants of the same tale." He is ready to accept only one complete folktale, which was recited as such, from Greek and Roman antiquity—the tale of Cupid and Psyche, told by an old woman in the robber's cave in the novel of Apuleius, and a very few other instances where stories told by the Greeks and Romans are identical in plot with modern folktales—the Polyphemus story, for example. He admits, of course, that single incidents and general ideas are common enough. So Thompson, though in *The Folktale* he has assembled over fifty motifs from classical literature, seems willing to consider only two series as close to complete oral narratives. These two appear in the Odes—the story of Perseus, treated by Pindar in greatly condensed form, and the story of the Argonauts, the longest of his mythical narratives. Of the Perseus story Thompson says: "The supernatural birth of the hero (T511), his abandonment and persecution along with his mother (S301), the theft of the single eye belonging to the Phorcides (K333.2), the overcoming of Medusa in spite of her power of turning people into stone through her glance (D581), and, finally, the winning of the princess Andromeda as a prize for defeating the sea monster to whom she was to be sacrificed (T68.1), all show us that we are here very close to a narrative form and to narrative material familiar to us in the modern folktale of the European peasant."[113] He thus accepts, partially at least, the conclusions in a three-volume study, *The Legend of Perseus* by Hartland, who "equated this legend with the present-day folktale of The Dragon Slayer and its related tale, The Two Brothers." Halliday, on the other hand, agrees with Bolte and Polívka that Hartland has failed in his main purpose—the resemblances are of too vague and general an order.[114]

The ambiguities in Pindar's condensation of the Perseus story (*Pyth.* XII. 7-22) have already been discussed. Perhaps questionable is Bowra's belief that the details of Apollodorus' narrative—especially the magic pouch and sandals—were perhaps derived from Pindar; but that Pindar knew the tale in its entirety may with confidence be assumed from his statement in *Nemean*

X. 4: "Long is the tale of Perseus and the Gorgon Medusa." Additional reference to the story is also probably made in the fragmentary *Dithyramb* IV. 70c, where Hermes is named as helper as well as Athena, and there is a clear reference to the people "who were made stone." In his scattered references the poet omits all mention of well-known features of the tale—the prison (tower) where Danae was confined, and the exposure of child and mother in the floating chest. The romantic episode of the freeing of Andromeda from the dragon also does not appear, perhaps because its character did not make it especially appropriate for an ode of victory. Thompson in his summary of motifs in the story might have included tower and floating chest, magic pouch and sandals.

Thompson also comments on the "considerable series of folktale motifs" which appear in the tale of the Argonauts. "Phrixos and Helle," he explains, "flee from the persecutions of their stepmother, as in several modern tales (cf. Type 450). . . . In Jason's fellow voyagers is to be found a good example of a very popular motif, that of the extraordinary companions. In a part of the Argonauts story, that dealing with Jason and Medea, we have many interesting parallels to one of the most widespread of modern European tales, The Girl as Helper on the Hero's Flight (Type 313). As in that tale, Medea, through her magic power, helps Jason perform the impossible tasks which have been assigned by her father."[115] There are additional motifs in the story, which appear in Pindar—the prophecy about the one-sandaled man, the ghost of Phrixus, and the Clashing Rocks, though Pindar omits the Obstacle Flight of the lovers, as well as many other incidents of the fully developed ancient tale, such as the visit to Phineus, the Harpies, and the sowing of the dragon's teeth in Aeëtes' field. But Halliday again shows some skepticism about regarding the flight of Medea and Jason as a variant of Grimm 79: "The rationalization has effected a pretty extensive change."[116]

To these two tales might be added the attempts of Mannhardt to show the folktale counterparts of the tales of Peleus at Acastus' court and his wooing of the sea-nymph Thetis, stories which may, with difficulty, be reconstructed from the glancing lyrical treatment of Pindar. We may see traces of "The Dragon Slayer" tale (Aarne-Thompson, Type 300) or perhaps of The Hunter (Type 304) in Pindar's brief allusions to Peleus' visit at the court of King Acastus in *Nemeans* IV and V.[117] Frazer calls the story "The Wicked Wife and the Virtuous Hero." It reads, he says, "like a fairy tale, and we can hardly doubt that it contains elements of genuine folk-lore." He then refers to W. Mannhardt's study and reconstruction of the tale, which first brought the background narrative to attention.[118] The details which Pindar gives in the two Odes are as follows: Hippolyte, Acastus' queen, conceives a passion for the young hero; he rejects her, and she accuses him to her husband, who, perhaps with her aid, plans revenge (Potiphar's Wife motif); the plan somehow involves Peleus' magic knife; Chiron comes to his aid and he, in turn, takes his revenge on Acastus by capturing and destroying Iolcus, his capital. The complete story may be pieced out from fragments of Hesiod (Pindar would certainly have known Hesiod's account), from Apollodorus, and from various scholiasts. According to Hesiod, Acastus planned to hide the magic knife Hephaestus had given Peleus (under dung, Apollodorus), so that the hero, in hunting for it would be slain by the savage beasts (Hesiod; centaurs, Apollodorus) who roamed the mountains. The other sources speak of Acastus' challenge to a hunting contest at which Peleus was to be discredited and abandoned; Peleus, however, craftily cut out the tongues of the animals he had slain as evidence of his skill, and was rescued by Chiron though he had fallen asleep in the forest.[119] It is interesting to note that the two details which have most of the flavor of popular tales—the cutting out of the tongues and the hiding of the knife in dung—Pindar omits, emphasizing instead, more in the epic vein, the hero's steadfast virtue and his capture of Iolcus single-handed, perhaps with the spear he himself had cut on Mount Pelion.[120]

The rest of the Peleus story which follows on this—his winning the Nereid Thetis for his bride (again a tale full of folklore motifs, some of which Pindar omits) —has already been discussed.[121] A little remains to be told of the Centaurs, those creatures "undoubtedly derived from popular belief," who figure so largely in this story.[122] It is apparent that Pindar was well-versed in the tales of these shaggy half-beast, half-man creatures who dwelt in the mountains of Thessaly. He refers to the origin of their race in the story of Ixion, and the Caeneus fragment indicates that he treated their battle with the Lapiths. His fondness for the wise Centaur Chiron, evidenced by the affectionate folklore touch in the title he gives him—"the divine beast"—appears in many scattered references throughout the Odes.[123] He must have known, since it appears early in literature, the story of Philyra, mother of Chiron, and her pursuit by Cronus in the form of a horse.[124] (Frazer characterizes a similar story of Demeter and Poseidon as "one of the most savage stories in Greek mythology"),[125] but Pindar chooses to disregard it entirely, and presents instead a picture of blissful family life in the famous cave, where Chiron, his wife, mother, and virtuous daughters lived, the friends and helpers of baby Jason and young Achilles. Chiron was tutor and adviser to Peleus and Asclepius, too, and once, with tongue in cheek perhaps, gives the desired prophecy on a love-affair to the god of prophecy himself.[126]

More significant because readily providing a series of motifs that give evidence of some unified narrative behind them is the tale of the quarrel of the Apharetidae (Idas and Lynceus) with the Dioscuri (Castor and Polydeuces), which Pindar tells at some length in *Nemean* X. The fact that twins are engaged in conflict with twins gives at once the flavor of folklore, since adventures of twin heroes are popular features of storytelling in all parts of the world; the North American Indian tales show several of these.[127] In this case we are close to the folklore material of Laconia or Messenia, though some details of the story appeared in the *Cypria*.[128] The quarrel was over "some trouble about cattle," as Pindar says vaguely, probably slurring over in this way the actual cause—a cattle raid and the subsequent cheating in an eating contest by one of the four participants. Apollodorus gives the details "in broad folklore more rustic than Chevy Chase," as Farnell puts it.[129] The two sets of twins had carried out a successful cattle raid, and Idas was appointed to distribute the spoils. He divided one of the carcasses into four equal parts, and proposed an eating contest, the side which finished first to have the booty. He consumed his portion first, then finished off his brother's, whereupon the two made off with all the cattle and the Dioscuri angrily followed to win them back. These details Pindar omitted as perhaps too undignified for his treatment. But other folklore features follow. Polydeuces and his brother hide in a hollow oak tree (it is remarkable how often the hollow tree is a hiding place in folktale narratives),[130] and Lynceus, who was gifted with magical sight which enabled him to see through solid objects,[131] spotted them in the trunk from the top of Mt. Taygetus. Then came the hand-to-hand encounter with the hurling of the gravestone (the combat took place near the tomb of Aphareus with its sinister associations),[132] and the thunder-clap of Zeus "in that lonely place" which killed the two sons of Aphareus. Castor, the mortal one of the Dioscuri, was already succumbing to a fatal wound when Polydeuces found him. Grief-stricken, the immortal twin prays that he may meet death with his brother, and Zeus permits them to share alternate life and death. If, in interpreting the difficult last line of the Ode, it is Polydeuces who "opened the eyes of Castor," we have again a folklore motif—that of magic resuscitation by the hero. This whole story, with its strong flavor of folklore motifs, might well deserve the attention of those interested in popular tales.

Summary

A glance at the motifs listed at the end of this investigation makes it clear that the number of folktale motifs in Pindar alone far exceeds Thompson's modest claim that the number he assembled in *The Folktale* (about fifty) would be doubled by a survey of all Greek literature and art.[1] Though there are some overlappings, the motifs here listed run into the hundreds. And because of the very nature of the allusive lyric style many more underlie the expressly narrated stories and might be added to the total. For it is evident that Pindar relied on the knowledge of his audience, taking it for granted that they knew the rich background of many of the tales. "Time presses; I know a short way," he says in the fourth *Pythian* when Jason has slain the dragon guarding the Fleece, and in rapid fashion he then sketches the rest of the story, telling how Jason stole away Medea "to be the death of Pelias." It is clear that he knows (and takes it for granted his audience knows) about Medea's feigned rejuvenescence of Pelias and its fatal results.[2] A more striking example of stories taken for granted concerns the fifty daughters of Danaus, who were commanded by their father to murder their bridegrooms on the wedding night. All obeyed except Hypermnestra, who "kept in the scabbard her sword of single-minded resolve." This last detail is the only one Pindar gives, considering the preliminaries of the story well known (*Nem.* X. 6). Again, when he refers to the later bride-race set by the same Danaus for his daughters' hands, much must be supplied: the girls were shunned because of the murders, and the father finds this way to secure new husbands for them (*Pyth.* IX. 112). In the

99

last passage the number of daughters is given as forty-eight, but this involves no inconsistency. The scholiast enlightens us by saying that Hypermnestra was omitted since her marriage to Lynceus was recognized, and another daughter, Amymone, was considered wed to Poseidon, who had rescued her from the advances of a satyr.[3] When Pindar rejects the common version of a story and substitutes one of his own, or hints at the truth in a "hush passage," the number of motifs is further increased.

Literary sources, as far as they can be traced, have been adequately treated by the editors and commentators. The absence of material from Homer is often mentioned. "To Homer, as the author of the *Iliad* and the *Odyssey*, he owes almost nothing" is Bowra's comment. However, the charge of "anti-Homeric bias" once applied to him is manifestly exaggerated.[4] It derives chiefly from the absence of allusions and from the passage in the Odes (*Nem.* VII. 21) in which Pindar is vindicating Ajax against the unfair judgment of the Greek army which favored Odysseus in the famous Contest of Arms. "Homer's sweet song has beguiled men so that Odysseus has won fame beyond his deserts," he says, but the statement seems intended as a tribute to the power of poetry rather than as a criticism of Homer. Indeed in another passage (*Isth.* IV. 37) he admits that the prowess of Ajax has been widely proclaimed by Homer. It is natural enough that Pindar should not attempt to treat material so well known as the Homeric, though his vocabulary, and above all the spirit of heroic achievement that breathes through the Odes, owes its inspiration to the great poet. As for Odysseus, he was plainly not a hero after Pindar's heart, nor one especially suitable for emulation in songs addressed to athletes.

Influence of the poems of the Epic Cycle, the *Aethiopis,* the *Little Iliad,* and others, is apparent; Bowra and Farnell have enumerated many instances. Hesiodic influence, especially in the choice of myths from the early period of mythology, has already been noted. Farnell repeatedly calls Hesiod Pindar's "master," and it is natural that a Boeotian predecessor should have weight, though it seems strange that Hesiod, the peasants' poet, should have had much influence on the aristocratic Pindar, and a considerable case could be built up of modifications and rejections of crudities in Hesiod's narratives.

Apart from such literary sources, Wilamowitz has filled in the background of folk beliefs in Boeotia at considerable length, stressing Pindar's avoidance of many of the crudities.[5] He mentions a serpent-cult, which may throw some light on the common story of Cadmus' transformation to a snake; the hand-to-hand conflict of the two rough mountain giants, Helicon and Cithaeron, which Pindar's countrywoman, Corinna, treated; and such grotesque figures as the goddess Hippo, who, in horse-form, roamed the mountain forests and brought aid to women in distress. In particular he mentions the horse-form of the god Poseidon, shown in such myths as those of the god's union with Melanippe (black mare), who bore him Boiotus, ancestor of the Boeotians, and with Demeter, who bore the wonder steed Arion. Though Poseidon, worshipped at Onchestus, figures prominently in Pindar's poetry (his connection with the horse is recognized by the epithet *Damios* [Tamer of Horses], by his gift of winged steeds to Pelops, and by

Bellerophon's sacrifice to him), the poet omits such grotesque stories current in his time. Amphion and Zethus, too, the Dioscuri of Thebes, born on Mt. Cithaeron, were known as the "white colts."

In spite of such omissions, not enough stress has been laid on Pindar's interest in local legends and folktales, though the probability of such sources was early recognized, as Croiset's discussion shows. Bowra refers several times to oral sources and has listed a number of Pindar's myths which he thinks were local in origin—those of Corinth, Rhodes, Cyrene, the account of the childhood of Achilles, and perhaps the story of Orestes.[6] In the notes of Farnell, about forty references may be found in which he sees the probable influence of folklore and local themes. Such influence may be suspected especially in little-known myths, such as those of Euxantius, Melia, Tenerus, and the Moliones. It is interesting to note that the detailed description of the "paved way" in Cyrene, with the tomb of Battus at "the far end by the marketplace" (*Pyth.* V. 92-93), seems to indicate an actual visit of Pindar to the city. Pausanias testifies to his inquiring of the inhabitants of Anthedon details of the story of Glaucus the "fisherman," who, after eating magic grass, leaped into the sea and became a sea-god.[7] In view of such evidence of the poet's interest in local tales some peculiarities of his treatment may be explained—why, for example, he gives praise in his summary of famous myths of Corinth to Sisyphus, usually classed as an arch-sinner; why Heracles is once described as small in stature; why Otus and Ephialtes and Tityus are used as complimentary references in the townspeople's praises of Jason. It is true, as Farnell puts it, that one should not look for consistency in a poet's treatment,[8] especially

102

as the period of the Odes stretches over many years, but the use of local legends in compliment to the victors celebrated would go far to explain many of these inconsistencies.

It is apparent that Pindar as a poet shows a liking for the unusual and the surprising (Bowra uses the word "fantastic"),[9] for the motifs in this index that in Thompson's scheme stress the supernatural and the primitive are the heavily weighted ones. So the chapters on Mythological Motifs (A), Extraordinary Animals (B), Magic (D), and Marvels (F) are well filled in contrast to the later ones such as Shift of Fortune (N), Society (P), Unnatural Cruelty (S), and the like. But even some of these later categories contain much of the supernatural: prophecies, in Ordaining the Future (M), are given through the unique device of the oracle, where the god's voice and presence are clearly realized, and the marriages of gods with mortal women take up much of Chapter T, Sex.

The direct comparison of the Indian tales with Pindar's was rewarding in that it showed how the primitive character of many of the motifs was clearly recognizable, though it had been modified. In the hero tales in particular striking similarities appear in these topics: unusual birth of the hero, tasks set by hostile relatives, conflicts with monstrous animals, assistance from animals, bride-winning, journeys of heroes, revenge taken on adversaries. The chief differences are in the means used to defeat the adversary—the use of trickery and magic (unless the help of the gods is so classified)—which the Greek mind and Greek morality (at least in Pindar) rejected. As we have seen, the main characteristics of the Indian tales are the predominance of magic (most often self-

103

transformation), dominance of the animal world, approval and use of trickery, and a general lack of systematization in the accounts of the gods and the formation and features of the earth. Consideration of the Heracles and Trickster myths raised questions of further possibly significant comparisons.

In many ways Pindar fitted the fantastic features of folklore into the more civilized attitudes of his day and the grand style appropriate to odes of victory. Instead of magic the presence of the gods gives a perpetual sense of wonder, and to Pindar's ardent religious spirit nothing prevents belief in the gods' miracles. "No act of the gods," he says in *Pythian* X. 48, "seems incredible." The gods appear in every one of the Odes, and they are present much more vividly than in occasional appearances to men or in the assistance they sometimes render, as characters in their own right and with their own interests. In many of these instances they speak as well as act, thus adding to the dramatic nature of the presentation. A striking example is the appearance of the king of the gods himself on the thunderstruck mountainside where Castor is dying. He speaks directly to his son Polydeuces in answer to that hero's anguished prayer, and gives him the chance of saving his brother by relinquishing half of his own immortality.

In other ways besides the semi-rationalization of terming all miracles the work of the gods, Pindar modifies the more fantastic features of folklore. Bowra, in his appraisal of Pindar, once describes him as "not averse from horrors and atrocities."[10] He goes on to analyze the scene of Pelops' dismemberment, when, according to the popular story, Tantalus was serving up his son to the gods to trick them in a cannibal feast. He also mentions Heracles' fierce attack on Antaeus, and cites a realistic description of the crunching of bones when that hero throws Diomede, the Thracian, to his flesh-eating mares. But when we consider the number of myths with savage features which Pindar modified, these few instances do not seem important enough to dwell on or term characteristic of the poet. We have already mentioned the omission of the cruel death inflicted by Ixion on his father-in-law, the murder of Phocus, the slaying of their bridegrooms by the Danaids, and the gruesome circumstances back of Athena's gift of immortality to Tydeus' son Diomede. Many other instances of such omissions have been noted. Indeed one might venture to say that the encomiastic nature of the Odes, celebrating successes of the athletes always, sets the tone for the mythical narratives as well.

In a more positive way Pindar softens the irrationalities by putting the heroic achievements in remote places and surrounding them with the romantic atmosphere of distance and loneliness—Hyperboreans in the far North, the Argonauts carrying their ship over the desolate ridges of Africa to meet a "lonely" god, the Pillars of Heracles at the ends of trackless seas in the gloom beyond Cadiz; next, by treating the miracles close at hand with touches of beauty and splendor—gold showers at the begetting of a hero or the birth of a goddess, sudden nighttime epiphanies of the great sea-god or of Zeus, appearing "close at hand," and everywhere the gleam of gold, and dazzling epithets of the gods recalling, yet often strikingly changed from, Homer's.[11] Evadne's crimson girdle and silver urn are pictured and her child Iamus lying bathed in the golden and purple light of pansy-flowers; the wings of the sons of Boreas

105

tremble and gleam with purple; and even the terrible dragon that Jason slays has gleaming eyes and spangled back in addition to his tremendous size. Size indeed is the thing the poet often stresses instead of abnormalities —the mighty Nemean lion, Alcyoneus, huge as a mountain, the monster Typhon (though in one place he does endow him with a hundred heads). The deformities of such creatures as the double-joined Moliones and triple-formed Geryon, the "daemon" of the West, are omitted; even the Gorgon is once described as "fair-cheeked." One has but to glance at the *Theogony* of Hesiod to see how these grotesque creatures have been modified in description. "The charming often renders the incredible credible," the poet himself explains in *Olympian* I. 32, in speaking of Pelops' gleaming ivory shoulder. The scholiasts occasionally express contempt for some of these touches, calling them products of Pindar's "fantastic imagination"—for example, when he speaks of the Clashing Rocks as being "stilled in death"[12]—or retires Pegasus to the "ancient stalls of Zeus." Modern critics, too, often strain to find precedents and parallels for similar fanciful touches, which should simply add testimony to the originality and genius of a great poet.

Farnell has termed these Epinicians "epic-lyric"—a phrase reminiscent of Quintilian's description of Stesichorus,[13] who "sustained the weight of epic with his lyre." The phrase has probably more to do with manner than with content, indicating the combination of dignified continuous narrative with lyric presentation in a succession of vivid scenes. Bowra, mentioning Alcman as Pindar's predecessor, has more specifically named four elements which Epinician Odes traditionally inherited —prayers or praise of the gods, myths from the heroic past, maxims, and personal remarks about poet or patron.[14] Pindar himself seems to allude to three of these in his question at the beginning of the second *Olympian:* "What god, what hero, what man shall we sing?" These apparently constitute what he calls elsewhere his *tethmos,* the laws governing his composition (*Nem.* IV. 33). With the maxims and personal reflections (which owe more to lyric than to epic influence) this investigation has had nothing to do, though mention might well be made of the animal figures which frequently accompany the maxims and illustrate them. The polypus that clings to a rock and changes color with its surroundings carries a moral easily deduced (*Fr.* 235B), as does the cock, brave only in its own yard (*Ol.* XII. 14). Burton, speaking of the closing section of *Pythian* II, remarks: "Pindar borrows his ideas from the world of the beast fable with its mixed population of the children's pet ape, the crafty fox, the fawning dog, and the wolf. He imagines himself and his enemies behind these animal masks even as Archilochus masked himself and his victims behind his fox, his ape, and his hedgehog."[15] The famous pair of crows of *Olympian* II. 87, who chatter in vain "against the godlike bird of Zeus" (taken by the scholiasts and some modern critics to represent Pindar's rivals, Simonides and Bacchylides)[16] seem to carry a personal and bitter significance. However this may be, these references to birds and animals, quite unlike the animal similes of the *Iliad,* seem definitely to belong as much to the inheritance of folklore as does that industrious ant held up as a reproach to sluggards in the Book of Proverbs. In one instance Farnell detects a "lowering of the epic style"— the "wryneck" incident in the story of the Argonauts.[17]

Summary

This seems not to be in the fashion of the older epic, but to look ahead to later erotic treatments of the Hellenistic age. The choice of the love story of Apollo and Cyrene, with its long analysis of the feelings of the god, as the chief myth of *Pythian* IX, seems again to show this same tendency. But all these elements have been skillfully fitted into the traditional framework of the Odes. The poet himself has described the complex texture well in *Pythian* I. 81, when he refers to himself as "drawing together the strands of many themes into brief compass."

Notes

Snell's numbering of the Fragments has been used throughout this book unless otherwise noted.

INTRODUCTION

1. J. H. Finley, *Pindar and Aeschylus* (Cambridge, Mass., 1955), pp. 93, 160.

2. C. M. Bowra, *Pindar* (Oxford, 1964), chap. III, pp. 99-158.

3. *Nem.* I. 33; *Pyth.* IX. 87.

4. Bowra, *Pindar,* pp. 283 and 285, refers to *Pyth.* I. 94, *Nem.* VI. 30, *Ol.* VII. 54-55 ("hearsay"), *Nem.* III. 52-53 ("oral tradition").

5. Stith Thompson, *The Folktale* (New York, 1951), p. 423. *Folklore,* 1890 (English journal published earlier as *Folk-Lore Record,* 1878-82, and *Folk-Lore Journal,* 1883-89); *Communications of the Folklore Fellows,* 1907.

6. H. M. and N. K. Chadwick, *The Growth of Literature* (Cambridge, 1932-40), III, 757. Cf. I, 181 ff.

7. Gilbert Murray, *Rise of the Greek Epic* (3rd ed., London, 1924), chap. V, "The Expurgations," pp. 120-145.

8. *The Folktale,* p. 280.

9. L. R. Farnell, *The Works of Pindar,* translated with Literary and Critical Commentaries, 2 vols. (London, 1930 and 1932).

10. *Rise of the Greek Epic,* p. 263, n. 1.

11. *The Folktale,* pp. 297-363.

12. Stith Thompson, *Tales of the North American Indians* (Cambridge, Mass., 1929); Tristram P. Coffin, *Indian Tales of North America* (Philadelphia, 1961); Susan Feldmann, *The Story Telling Stone: Myths and Tales of the American Indians* (New York, 1965), and her *African Myths and Tales* (New York, 1963); John Greenway, *The Primitive Reader* (Hatboro, Pa., 1965); K. Langloh Parker, *Australian Legendary Tales* (Sydney, 1953).

13. *Pyth.* X. 53.

14. *The Folktale,* pp. 33, 329-344 *passim*; A. H. Krappe, *The Science of Folk-Lore* (London, 1930), pp. 16-25; Jan de Vries, *Heroic Song and Heroic Legend* (London, 1963), pp. 210-226, "The Pattern of an Heroic Life."

15. W. R. Halliday, *Greek and Roman Folklore* (New York, 1927), p. 74. See also his *Indo-European Folk-Tales and Greek Legend* (Cambridge, 1933), pp. 10-12.

16. *Race, Language, and Culture* (New York, 1940, p. 405.

17. Stith Thompson, "Myths and Folktales," in *Myth, A Symposium,*

edited by Thomas A. Sebeok (Bloomington, Indiana, 1955), p. 107.
Susan Feldmann, *The Story Telling Stone,* p. 36.

18. J. R. R. Tolkien, *Tree and Leaf* (Boston, 1965), pp. 23, 24.

HERO-TALE MOTIFS

1. *Literature among the Primitives* (Hatboro, Pa., 1964), chap. VIII, "The Scholars," pp. 270-295. Greenway illustrates and expands his study in a companion volume, *The Primitive Reader,* which he describes as an anthology of tales, songs, riddles, and proverbs from aboriginal peoples around the world. Other recent publications on folklore are *The Anthropologist Looks at Myth,* compiled by Melville Jacobs and edited by Greenway (Austin, 1966)—a collection of papers by scholars particularly interested in the role of verbal art in modern anthropology —and *The Study of Folklore* by Alan Dundes (Englewood Cliffs, N.J., 1965), which contains a comprehensive series of articles on definitions, search for origins, form, transmission, and functions of folklore with concise critical introductions, much bibliographical material, and suggestions for further study. The introductory essay in M. J. and F. E. Herskovits' *Dahomean Narrative* (Evanston, Ill., 1958) also contains a summary and criticism of Freudian, Jungian, Ritualistic and other methods of explaining myths. The authors conclude that no one of them provides a complete answer, and stress the point that myth must be regarded as a manifestation of human culture along with the factor of borrowing and the creative drive in man. They make a strong plea for "cross-culture" studies.

2. "The Biographical Pattern in Traditional Narrative," *Journal of the Folklore Institute,* I (1964), no. 1/2, 114-129.

3. *The Hero: A Study in Tradition, Myth, and Drama* (New York, 1937).

4. *Literature among the Primitives,* pp. 103-105.

5. *The Folktale,* pp. 339-344. Katherine Spencer, *Mythology and Values: An Analysis of Navaho Chantway Myths* (Philadelphia, Pa., 1957), p. 21.

6. *Tales of the North American Indians,* no. XLIV, p. 104. Greek heroes, birth of Perseus, *Pyth.* XII. 17; Heracles, *Isth.* VII. 5; childhood feat: Heracles, *Nem.* I. 33 ff.; Achilles, *Nem.* III. 43 ff.

7. *Pyth.* IV. 114 ff.

8. *The Folktale,* p. 116. The psychoanalytical mythologists make much of this hostility of relatives. See *Myth and Mythmaking,* edited by Henry A. Murray (New York, 1960), essay 2: "Recurrent Themes in Myths and Mythmaking," by Clyde Kluckhohn, pp. 52, 54; and

Notes on pages 11-15

Katherine Spencer, *op. cit.*, pp. 19, 35-36. Pindar stresses especially the relationship between Jason and Pelias in *Pyth.* IV.

9. *The Folktale*, p. 436. See also Axel Olrik's "Epic Laws of Folk Narrative" (translation) in Alan Dundes, *The Study of Folklore* (Englewood Cliffs, N.J., 1965), p. 133, for the Law of Three.

10. Rhys Carpenter, *Folktale, Fiction, and Saga in the Homeric Epics* (Berkeley, 1962), pp. 71, 173.

11. See especially nos. 1 and 3 in Susan Feldmann's *The Story Telling Stone*. For the establishment of the winds at the four quarters of the earth, see *The Folktale*, p. 315, and *Tales*, n. 266, p. 350.

12. T. B. L. Webster, *From Mycenae to Homer* (2nd. ed., New York, 1964), p. 67, says that the Chimera may be a fourteenth-century Hittite monster. References in Pindar: Lion, *Isth.* III. 12; Dragon, *Pyth.* IV. 245; Gorgon, *Pyth.* XII. 9; Chimera, *Ol.* XIII. 90; Cerberus, *Fr.* 249b (*Dith.* II); Typhon, *Ol.* IV. 7; Bulls, *Pyth.* IV. 225-26.

13. Webster, *ibid.*, p. 82, thinks the monster Huwawa that Gilgamesh encounters has a strong facial resemblance to the Gorgon. Pindar, visiting Sicily in 476 as the guest of Chromius of Aetna, may have seen the archaic metope of the temple at Selinus showing Pegasus' birth as Perseus cuts off Medusa's head.

14. Martin P. Nilsson, *The Mycenaean Origin of Greek Mythology* (New York, 1963), pp. 217-218.

15. Farnell, I, 161.

16. Ulrich von Wilamowitz-Moellendorff, *Pindaros* (Berlin, 1922), p. 256.

17. Lion, *Isth.* VI. 47-49; Deer, *Ol.* III. 29; Cerberus, *Fr.* 249b, *Dith.* II; Diomede, *Fr.* 169, 9; Geryon, *Isth.* I. 13. J. B. Bury, *The Isthmian Odes of Pindar* (London, 1892), note on *Isth.* I. 13, Orth(r)os, dog of Geryon: Pindar's plural is surprising, since in all the legends only one dog is mentioned. "The scholiast" continues Bury, "suggests that Pindar is given to exaggeration [quoting Hesiod's reference to one dog]. He adds that Pindar may have considered it unworthy of Heracles to confront him with a single dog. "We can understand that Pindar might have regarded the dog as in a certain sense plural" (since he is usually described as two-headed). So C. A. M. Fennell (*The Nemean and Isthmian Odes*, Cambridge, 1883) says on *Isth.* I. 13: "It must remain a question whether Orthros is made plural in consideration of his two heads or whether Pindar is following an unknown version of the myth." Höfer in Roscher, article on Orth(r)os, does not comment expressly on this unusual plural, though he does refer to the scholiast on *Isth.* I. 13 (15a, b). Vase paintings of the dog according to Höfer are of three types, showing him as a normal hound, or with two heads and a serpent's tail, or with three heads.

18. *Nem.* I. 62; *Nem.* III. 23; cf. *Isth.* IV. 57. There may be an allusion to the sea-beast which threatened Hesione in one or more of these passages. The scholiast on *Nem.* III. 23 (42a) says, "The assignment for the sea-monster—that one concerning Troy and Laomedon," and on *Nem.* I. 62 (96) a reference is made to *Iliad* XX. 146-147, to the sea-monster that threatened Troy. Webster, *From Mycenae to Homer,* p. 176, hazards a guess that a scene on a Geometric *kantharos* in Copenhagen shows Heracles' struggle with this sea-monster. He had to fight the monster from within its belly, and was bald on emerging (Hellanicus, quoted by the scholiast on Homer's *Iliad* XX. 146, and by Tzetzes on Lycophron, 34). A vase-painting gives evidence that there was a similar story about Jason and the Colchian dragon. Thompson in *The Folktale* (p. 343) gives amazing parallels from the North Pacific coast and from Siberia of the victims of swallowing becoming bald, as does Jan de Vries in *Heroic Song and Heroic Legend* (p. 218). Frazer (I, 211) on Apollod. II. 5. 10, n. 5: "Compare Diodorus Siculus, iv. 17. 3 *sq.,* who says that Hercules completely cleared Crete of wild beasts, and that he subdued many of the wild beasts in the deserts of Libya and rendered the land fertile and prosperous."

19. H. M. and N. K. Chadwick, *The Growth of Literature*, I, 205.

20. See Robert H. Lowie, "The Test Theme in North American Mythology," *Journal of American Folklore*, XXI (1908), 97-148. Thompson, *The Folktale:* sucking monster, p. 341; cliff ogre, p. 341; sharp-elbowed women, p. 342; burr-women, p. 342; cannibal giantess, p. 359; women wrestlers, p. 336; pot-tilter, p. 337; ogre with fire-sandals, p. 337.

21. Cycnus, *Ol.* X. 15; Antaeus, *Isth.* IV. 52; Geryon, *Isth.* I. 13, *Dith.* II, *Fr.* 169. 4; Moliones, *Ol.* X. 26-34; Alcyoneus, *Isth.* VI. 33; *Nem.* IV. 27; Porphyrion, *Pyth.* VIII. 12.

22. *Mycenaean Origins of Greek Mythology*, pp. 217-219.

23. Triple-bodied Geryon, Hesiod, *Theogony* 287; Moliones (Hesiod), H. J. Rose, *A Handbook of Greek Mythology* (New York, 1960), p. 219; Cycnus, Rose, *Mythology,* p. 233; Antaeus, Rose, *Mythology,* p. 67; Alcyoneus, Scholiast on Pindar, *Nem.* IV. 27 (43d).

24. Bacchylides 18. 28.

25. Thompson, *The Folktale,* p. 341.

26. See below, p. 97.

27. Nilsson, *Mycenaean Origin of Greek Mythology,* p. 217: "The opinion has been advanced that the cleaning of the stables of Augeias . . . is a late addition, but I am not sure that this view is right, for the myth has a folk-tale motif which agrees very well with a humorous conception of Heracles." See Thompson, *The Folktale,* p. 89, for the common task of cleaning dirty stables.

28. See above, n. 13.

29. Suidas, *Kerkopes*; Apollod. II. 6. 3; Diod. Sic. IV. 31. 7.

30. See Hesiod, *The Homeric Hymns, and Homerica,* edited and translated by H. G. Evelyn-White, 1920, pp. xl, 538; Rose, *Mythology,* p. 217 and notes; Roscher, *Lexikon,* II. 1166; *Kerkopen* by K. Seeliger.

31. The Monster-Slayers (Zuni) in *The Story Telling Stone,* no. 3, p. 47.

32. Greenway, *Literature among the Primitives,* pp. 76-79.

33. Symplegades motif; see Thompson, *Tales,* p. 275, n. 15, for a listing of many examples. In the story of Glooscap (p. 6), a "cloudy wall rose and fell at intervals, and struck the ground with such force that whatever was caught under it would be crushed to atoms; but the good could dart under when it rose, and come out on the other side unscathed." Thompson, *The Folktale:* snapping doors, p. 330; swooping trees, p. 337.

34. *Pyth.* IV. 209 ff.

35. Scholiast on *Pyth.* IV. 209 (370).

36. Farnell, II, 163, compares Apollodorus I. 9. 22 ff. and *Odyssey* XII. 61.

37. Hyginus, *Fab.* CXXV for Sirens; see *Fab.* XIX and notes for Symplegades, in *The Myths of Hyginus,* tr. and ed. by Mary Grant (Lawrence, 1960); Thompson, *Tales,* XLIV.

38. *Il.* XXII, 20.

39. Bowra, *Heroic Poetry* (London, 1952), pp. 125-126.

40. *Il.* V. 336. 858, *Od.* IV. 365 ff.

41. Webster, *From Mycenae to Homer,* p. 123.

42. Nilsson, *The Mycenaean Origin of Greek Mythology,* pp. 201, 202.

43. Lowie, "The Test Theme in North American Mythology," p. 134.

44. Thompson, *The Folktale,* pp. 314, 315, 330.

45. Fight with Scamander, *Il.* XXI; shooting at sun, Apollod. II. 5. 10. Frazer in his note on this passage says: "Apollodorus seems to be here following Pherecydes, as we learn from a passage which Athenaeus (xi. 39, p. 470 C D) quotes from the third book of Pherecydes as follows: 'And Hercules drew his bow at him as if he would shoot, and the Sun bade him give over; so Hercules feared and gave over.'" Later in the same passage of Pherecydes Heracles is about to shoot Ocean, and Ocean is afraid and bids him "give over." Typhon, mentioned above (see *Pyth.* I. 15 ff:), might offer another parallel here, since he plainly typifies destructive forces of nature, but gods rather than heroes are his subduers in the Greek tale. From another culture Jacob wrestling with the angel comes to mind.

46. *The Story Telling Stone,* Tlingit tale, no. 37, p. 204; Miao tale, "The Fearful Sun," p. 55.

47. *African Myths and Tales,* edited by Susan Feldmann, Intr., p. 26.

48. Theodor H. Gaster, *The Oldest Stories in the World* (New York, 1952), pp. 34-42, with comments; *Kalevala,* Runo XVI, "Tuonela"; *Odyssey* XI.

49. *The Story Telling Stone,* nos. 35 and 36, "The Man Who Brought his Wife Back from Spiritland," and "Coyote and Eagle Visit the Land of the Dead"; *Tales of the North American Indians,* no. LV, "Orpheus."

50. Wounding of Hades, *Ol.* IX. 29-36. See above, p. 20. For the possible treatment of Meleager in *Dith.* II, see especially *Fr.* 249a.

51. Thompson, *The Folktale,* pp. 345-352: *Tales of the North American Indians,* nos. LI, LV, LVI (Chief Echo); LX under water world; LXVI underworld of deer.

52. Mary Grant O'Sheridan, *Gaelic Folk Tales* (Chicago, 1909), Oisin in Tir-na-n-og, pp. 154-173.

53. Snell apparently does not consider that Strabo's statement (XV. 711: "Megasthenes [writing of India] agrees with Pindar, Simonides, and other story-tellers in his account of the Hyperboreans who live for a thousand years") is sufficient justification for including this in his volume of Fragments, as Bowra does. Bolton, too, is somewhat doubtful, for "the agreement may have only been about their way, not their length, of life" (p. 99 of *Aristeas of Proconnesus*). Yet Pindar himself (*Pyth.* X. 41) says they did not know age.

54. *Indian Tales of North America,* ed. Tristram P. Coffin, no. 23.

55. J. D. P. Bolton is interested in Pindar's account of the Hyperboreans because his placing the Gorgons near them is some indication that he was familiar with the *Arimaspea* of Aristeas. See *Aristeas of Proconnesus* (Oxford, 1962), pp. 71, 127. The name of Aristeas of Proconnesus appears in *Fragment* 271 of Pindar. In a long note (32 on pp. 195-196) Bolton sums up well the problems connected with the Hyperboreans "whose first appearance in Greek legend cannot be dated by other evidence before Aristeas" (p. 98). In this note Bolton speaks of ancient and modern attempts at etymologies, Alcaeus' *Hymn to Apollo,* the Hyperborean offerings to Delos, and the whole question as to the relationship of the legend to Delphi, concluding (p. 196): "I am disposed to incline to the view that Page says the evidence favours: that in origin the Hyperboreans are not a real people but a folk-memory— 'the earlier settlement of an Apollo who spread with his worshippers southward over the Greek mainland.' " For Abaris, Aristeas, and "soul-birds" see also E. R. Dodds, *The Greeks and the Irrational* (Berkeley, 1951), pp. 140-141 and notes.

56. Hesiod, *Works and Days*, 156-169. Bowra, *Pindar*, pp. 183-184, comments on Pindar's taste for myths with an element of war or violence in them: "In some respects the Games resemble war, and sometimes Pindar equates the two."

57. *Nem*. III. 34, Iolcus; *Fr*. 172, Fleece; *Nem*. III. 35, Thetis; *Fr*. 172, Troy. For Heracles, see his various Labors, and *Fr*. 172 again for Troy.

58. Thompson, *The Folktale*, p. 353.

59. Quoted with approval by Thompson, *The Folktale*, p. 381, from Lang's Introduction to Cox, *Cinderella*, pp. xi ff.

60. Tristram P. Coffin (*Indian Tales of North America*, Intr., p. xv) says: "The stories, with one or two exceptions, are set in an earlier era, when animals, birds, objects, forces of nature, and the like behaved as human beings behave. . . . Thus, the hero of any story may seem to be human at one moment and animal at the next. Coyote can howl at the moon and build a fire." Thompson, *The Folktale*, pp. 308, 309, 325.

61. *The Folktale*: lizard, p. 338; gopher, p. 338; bat, p. 339; mouse, p. 314; insect, p. 343. See also spider, p. 348; mole and badger, p. 358; crow, p. 355.

62. Halliday, *Greek and Roman Folklore*, pp. 87, 99, 100.

63. Apuleius, *The Golden Ass*, VI. 10, 15.

64. Rose, *Mythology*, pp. 290, 291; Grant, *The Myths of Hyginus, Poetica Astronomica*, II. 40; Sophie Trenkner, *The Greek Novella in the Classical Period* (New York, 1958), p. 48, n. 4, gives a reference to Stesichorus from Aelian (*N.A*. XVII. 37) in which an eagle prevents a man from drinking poison. Talking and helpful birds in ballad literature are treated by L. C. Wimberly, *Folklore in English and Scottish Ballads* (New York, 1965), pp. 44-52. Miss Trenkner, p. 10, gives several other examples of faithful animals, found chiefly in Aelian. Marital infidelity is the subject of most of these anecdotes, as in the story of Coronis referred to in the text below. *Argonautica* III. 927-937.

65. Oracular animals: cow to Thebes, Hyg. *Fab*. CLXXVIII, Apollod. III. 4. 1; ram to water, Hyg. *Fab*. CXXXIII; she-goat to Aegeae, Hyg. *Fab*. CCXIX; cow to Ilium, Apollod. III. 12. 3. For Arion see Paus. VIII. 25. 7 and VIII. 42. 1. In Statius (*Theb*. XI. 442) he prophesies to Adrastus the unlucky outcome of the campaign against Thebes. Propertius (II. 34. 37) calls him *vocalis*. Perhaps here and with the horses of Achilles the Greeks come nearest to the romantic association of hero and horse mentioned by Bowra in his *Heroic Poetry* (pp. 157-169).

66. *Iliad* XIX. 404 ff.

67. *Pyth*. IV. 161, 241. The ram in usual versions was sent by Zeus or by Hermes; Pindar does not specify. Pegasus, *Ol*. XIII. 64; *Isth*. VII. 44.

68. *Pyth.* III. 25 ff. and scholiast (52b). Bowra, *Pindar*, p. 60.

69. Thompson, *The Folktale*, p. 264; Rose, *Mythology*, pp. 288-290; Hyginus *Fab.* CCLII.

70. Thompson, *Tales of the North American Indians*, n. 146(b), p. 316.

71. *Nem.* III. 58; *Pyth.* VI. 22.

72. *The Folktale*, pp. 70-73.

73. Bowra, *The Greek Experience* (Cleveland, 1957), p. 108.

74. Bowra, *Heroic Poetry*, p. 91.

75. R. W. B. Burton, *Pindar's Pythian Odes* (Oxford, 1962), p. 29. Farnell, II, 235. For the Graeae (Phorcides) see Hyg. *Astr.* II. 12 following Aeschylus' *Phorcides*, and Apollod. II. 4. 2. with Frazer's notes. Halliday (*Indo-European Folk-Tales and Greek Legend*, p. 133) thinks the motif of Old, Older, Oldest may be recognized in the Perseus story, with the hero sent first to the aged Graeae, and then to the Nymphs for his equipment. Aeschylus (*Prometheus Bound*, 794-796) speaks of the Phorcides (Graeae) as aged swan-shaped maidens. In his comment on this passage, Bolton (*Aristeas of Proconnesus*, pp. 177-178) with reference to Gorgons and Graeae, says: "Aeschylus, in a significant context, locates them strangely, apparently in the north-east of the world (Pindar puts the Gorgons near the Hyperboreans): they live in darkness, and the Graeae are 'swan-shaped.' Central Asiatic lore knows of fierce and ugly 'swan maidens,' who live in Stygian darkness and can fly." It is an intriguing thought that there may be a parallel between the Greek Graeae and the swan-maidens of Indian and other cultures. Halliday, it is true, states (*Greek and Roman Folklore*, p. 91) that he does not know of an instance of the widely distributed Swan-Maiden motif in classical folklore, and Bolte-Polívka give no references to such, but the passage in Aeschylus stands, and Wimberly (*Folklore in the English and Scottish Ballads*, Intr., p. 16) gives encouragement to further investigation: "It would . . . be a mole-eyed type of scholarship to treat the incident, say, of the swan-maiden, as a purely literary incident and overlook the occurrence of this story in savage tradition." See no. LXXVI, "The Swan-Maidens," p. 198, in Thompson's *Tales of the North American Indians*, and the Cree tale of "Mudjikiwis" (no. LIV, p. 135 with n. 206) in *Tales*. It contains the Old, Older, Oldest motif and also the inexhaustible meat-pot *(Tischen-deck-dich)*. Pindar, with his placing the Graeae near the land of the Hyperboreans, may be of some service here. Pindar has two references to the petrification caused by Medusa's glance, *Pyth.* X. 46-48 and *Dith.* IV. 41. For parallels to the "death-glance" see no. 29, "Rolling Skull," in Coffin's *Indian Tales of North America*, and his prefatory note, and Thompson's *Tales*, pp. 344, 349.

76. Knife of Daedalus, *Nem.* IV. 59. This passage is in much dispute. Most accounts—and they are many, for it was a famous piece of equipment, whether knife or sword—state that it was made by Hephaestus. Attempts have been made consequently to equate Daedalus with Hephaestus (Snell? Bury, Bergk) or to make an adjective of the name—"finely-wrought" (Farnell). See the part played by the knife in the Tale-Type discussion, p. 95 below.

77. Athene and bridle, *Ol.* XIII. 65-66; Athene and Gorgon, *Pyth.* XII. 7; Aphrodite and iynx, *Pyth.* IV. 216; Poseidon and winged steeds, *Ol.* I. 86-87.

78. Peleus' spear, *Nem.* III. 33; Achilles' spear, *Nem.* VI. 54-55 (85b).

79. Wimberly, *Folklore in the English and Scottish Ballads*, pp. 89 ff.

80. Club, *Ol.* IX. 30; *Fr.* 111 (fight with Antaeus?); bow and arrows, *Isth.* VI. 33-35; *Pyth.* I. 52-53. The shield, so carefully described (*Shield of Heracles*) by Hesiod (?), is not part of his customary equipment.

81. *Isth.* VI. 35-49; Farnell, I, 267.

82. *Isth.* VI. 53, 54; Edward Clodd, *Magic in Names and in Other Things* (London, 1920), pp. 12, 65, 66 (the last two pages give Indian beliefs). See also Bowra, *Pindar,* pp. 211, 212.

83. Carpenter, *Folktale, Fiction, and Saga in the Homeric Epics,* p. 20.

84. Iolaus, *Pyth.* IX. 79; XI. 60; *Isth.* I. 16.

85. Patroclus, *Ol.* IX. 76-79; *Ol.* X. 16-19.

86. Thompson has listed magic objects occurring in his *Tales* on pp. 362-363.

87. Thompson, *The Folktale*, pp. 330, 331, 333, 335, 338.

88. *The Folktale*, p. 343. Thompson remarks, p. 334, that often the helpers are provided by the mother, whereas the father is often the opponent. For Medea, see p. 46 below.

89. *The Folktale,* pp. 319-328.

90. Paul Radin, *The Trickster: A Study in American Indian Mythology,* with commentaries by Karl Kerényi and C. G. Jung (London, 1956).

91. Kerényi, p. 188. Anansi the Spider is one of the chief tricksters in African tales (Feldmann, *African Myths and Tales,* p. 14).

92. Greenway, *Literature among the Primitives,* pp. 71-91.

93. Murray, *Rise of the Greek Epic,* pp. 93-94.

94. Hesiod, *Works and Days,* 59.

95. Murray, *Rise of the Greek Epic,* p. 85.

96. Rose, *Mythology,* p. 270, for Sisyphus.

97. W. C. Wright, *Short History of Greek Literature* (New York, 1907), p. 129.

98. *Nem.* VII. 20 ff. See below, p. 49.

99. *Nem.* III. 35-36; *Nem.* IV. 62-64.

100. See below, p. 100. According to Murray again (*Rise of the Greek Epic,* p. 274), the old pre-Hellenic strain of beliefs and emotions re-emerged after the decline of the epos. In Hesiod and Theognis and in tragedy such themes are common enough. Sophie Trenkner (*The Greek Novella in the Classical Period,* p. 46) stresses the use of intrigue by Euripides, and speaking of the Euripidean hero's view of life, describes it as "similar to the theories supported by certain sophists, which is at the same time that of folklore, in which it is honorable to achieve success by trickery."

101. Tantalus, *Ol.* I. 59; Coronis, *Pyth.* III. 25 ff.; Laomedon, *Nem.* III. 36; *Isth.* VI. 29; Clytemnestra, *Pyth.* XI. 17; Ixion, *Pyth.* II. 21; Moliones, *Ol.* X. 34; Graeae? *Pyth.* XII. 13.

102. *The Folktale,* p. 326.

103. Neoptolemus, *Pyth.* I. 50; Pelops, *Ol.* I. 86 ff.

104. Dioscuri, *Nem.* X. 60 ff. Bowra, *Pindar,* p. 300.

105. A curious treatment is given the arch-trickster, Sisyphus, in *Ol.* XIII. 52. He is praised for his "wise counsel," as he is apparently praised for craft in the *Iliad* (VI. 153), and even *Ol.* I. 60 may contain no allusion to his everlasting punishment. See n. 60 on Part II. Pindar may be following Corinthian folklore in the *Olympian* XIII passage. His part in betraying the love affair between Zeus and Aegina (Rose, *Mythology,* p. 294) is never mentioned, though there are many references in the Odes to this love. The poet also discounts the story of Tantalus' attempted deceit of the gods in serving up his son Pelops at a banquet, though he accepts the story of his theft of nectar and ambrosia, *Ol.* I. 60 ff.

106. Karl Kerényi, Part IV, "The Trickster in Relation to Greek Mythology," of Paul Radin's *The Trickster,* p. 176.

107. *Isth.* I. 12; *Fr.* 29. 4; *Nem.* I. 56-58; "lawless creatures": *Nem.* I. 61-66; *Isth.* IV. 57-60; *Nem.* III. 23.

108. Bowra, *Pindar,* pp. 74-76.

109. Farnell, II, 471 and 15; I, 352. See on this passage W. C. Greene, *Moira: Fate, Good, and Evil in Greek Thought,* and Martin Ostwald, "Pindar, *Nomos,* and Hercules," *Harvard Studies in Classical Philology,* LX (1965), 109-138.

110. Richard M. Dorson, "Theories of Myth and the Folklorist," p. 83, in Henry A. Murray, *Myth and Mythmaking.*

111. Tristram P. Coffin, *Indian Tales of North America,* p. xvi.

112. Franz Boas, "Mythology and Folktales of the North American Indians," *Journal of American Folk-Lore,* XXVII (1914), 395. Greenway, *Literature among the Primitives,* p. 90.

113. Interesting questions arise about Heracles and his Labors, apart from Pindar's treatment. Was he originally a Master Thief, as Sophie Trenkner assumes? (*The Greek Novella in the Classical Period*, p. 88, n. 3.) Five of the Labors imply theft: the Apples of the Hesperides, the Cattle of Geryon, the Horses of Diomedes, the Girdle, Cerberus. When did the trick of shifting the sky to Atlas come into the Hesperides story? Did he at first clean the stables of Augeas by hand, as the fifth-century metope at Olympia shows? Eurystheus did not "count" this Labor, if done by the trick of the rivers, nor that of the Hydra, if Iolaus helped him, as he did not perform them according to the agreement, with his own hands. (Rose, *Mythology*, p. 216, and n. 126 on p. 227.)

114. Thompson, *The Folktale:* Boas collection, p. 331; Dirty Boy, p. 337; Son-in-Law tests, pp. 90, 329, 333; Swan Maiden, p. 350. The tale "Dirty Boy" is no. XLVIII in Thompson's *Tales.* See also Tale no. XLVI, The Son-In-Law Tests.

115. *Ol.* I. 67-89.

116. *Pyth.* IX. 105 ff. Pindar may also have told the story of Heracles' wrestling with Dejanira's suitor, the bull-formed river-god Achelous, and the wrenching off of his horn, *Fr.* 249a.

117. *Nemean* IV. 62-65; *Nem.* III. 35; and below, p. 95.

118. Apollod. III. 13. 5, Frazer's notes and his Appendix X, for the Cretan story. J. C. Lawson, *Modern Greek Folklore and Ancient Greek Religion* (Cambridge, 1910), pp. 136-137, for the Messenian story. In both these there are two points of resemblance to the ancient tale, as Lawson points out: the changes to beasts and to fire, and the advice to hold fast (given by an old woman in the modern tales, and by Chiron in the ancient one). Frazer discusses the relation of the Peleus-Thetis story to the Swan-Maiden type of tale also in his *Appendix.*

119. *Isth.* VIII. 26-47; *Nem.* V. 26-37.

120. Farnell, II, 474. In Hesiod's account, Zeus, out of spite to Hera, humiliates Thetis by giving her to a mortal. See *Catalogues of Women,* 57, and Evelyn-White's translation of Hesiod, p. 185.

121. Joseph Campbell, *The Hero with a Thousand Faces* (New York, 1949), pp. 109-120, makes "meeting with the goddess" an important point in the outline of his psychologically conceived "Monomyth"—the "ultimate adventure," the "mystical marriage with the queen goddess of the world"—but Greek mythology does not easily respond to such classifications. The Andromeda episode in the Perseus story is considered by some scholars (see Halliday, *Indo-European Folk-Tales and Greek Legend,* p. 119) to be but a secondary adventure to the Gorgon-slaying. Heracles does not win a princess for his performance of the Twelve Labors, nor does Achilles for his prowess at Troy (ex-

119

cept after death?); both Theseus and Jason accept help gratefully, but desert their helpers. Campbell's citing as a parallel (p. 119) the Arapaho tale in which the girl is enticed by Porcupine to mount a stretching tree and win a supernatural mate (Thompson, *Tales*, no. LI) omits the ending of the story with the girl's immediate and persistent efforts to return to earth. Slight conformity with Campbell's idea may be seen in the divine marriages of Heracles and Cadmus.

122. *Pyth*. IV. 250.

123. Thompson, *Tales*, XLVI, p. 113. See Tale LIII, "The Arrow Chain," p. 131, for the Delayed Pursuit motif.

124. Thompson, *The Folktale*, Animal Wives and Husbands, pp. 353-358. Marriages to snakes, bears, buffalos, and deer are common in North American mythology, but common also are the themes of attempted escape from such unions.

125. *The Folktale*, pp. 332, 341, 334.

126. Pelias, *Pyth*. IV. 250; Augeas, *Ol*. X. 28, 41; Polydectes, *Pyth*. XII. 14; Oenomaus, *Ol*. I. 76, 88; Eurystheus, *Pyth*. IX. 81.

127. Orestes, *Pyth*. XI. 36. There has been much discussion about the relative dates of *Pyth*. XI and the Orestean trilogy of Aeschylus. Bowra (*Pindar*, pp. 402-405) puts the date of *Pyth*. XI in 454-3, thus four years after the *Agamemnon*; Farnell, II, xiv, leaves the matter undecided. C. H. Whitman (*Sophocles, A Study of Heroic Humanism* [Cambridge, 1951], p. 161), says that Sophocles and Pindar both were probably "in the main stream of tradition, when they omitted the Furies and treated the murders as simple justice. A Fury (Erinnys) appears but once in the Odes (*Ol*. II. 41) when she witnesses the murder of Laius and brings about the mutual slaying of Oedipus' sons.

128. Farnell, II, 471.

129. Thompson, *The Folktale*, pp. 264, 308, 311.

130. Heracles, *Nem*. I. 71; X. 18; *Isth*. IV. 59. Diomede, *Nem*. X. 7; Castor, *Pyth*. XI. 63-64; Cadmus and Peleus, *Ol*. II. 78; Achilles, *Ol*. II. 79, *Nem*. IV. 49. The curious passage in Euripides' *Bacchae* (1330-9) giving Dionysus' prediction of Cadmus' transformation to a snake and his ultimate bodily translation to Elysium has occasioned much discussion among the critics. Dodds (*Euripides' Bacchae*, n. on pp. 221-222) thinks the account in Euripides "bears traces of having been put together at a relatively late date out of heterogeneous older elements." The translation to Elysium "is the only part of the prophecy which Pindar knows (or, as a good Theban, chooses to mention), *Ol*. II. 78. It must originally have been alternative, not additional, to the snake story." Wilamowitz thought that a local snake god was identified by the Greeks with Cadmus (*Pindaros*, p. 37). Farnell states merely (II, 21) that Pindar's placing Cadmus in Elysium "clashes with the early

and widespread folk-saga of his snake transformation and burial in Illyria." Parallels to the snake-transformation motif may be seen in Susan Feldmann's *African Myths and Tales:* "The first human beings did not know death. When they grew old they were changed into snakes" (no. 50). "The god Ruwa had decreed that men should change their skins like the snake and become young when they had attained a great age" (no. 48). Such ideas may help to modify our reactions to the grotesqueness of the Euripidean passage.

131. Whitman, *Sophocles, A Study of Heroic Humanism.* See p. 70 for Ajax.

132. Neoptolemus, *Paean* VI. 102 ff. and *Nem.* VII. 35-43, 102-4; Bellerophon, *Ol.* XIII. 91, *Isth.* VII. 44-47; Ajax, *Nem.* VII. 26, VIII. 23-27; *Isth.* IV. 35. Wilamowitz (*Pindaros,* p. 374, n. 2) comments on the similarity of *Ol.* XIII. 92 and Euripides' *Bellerophon,* 312.

133. Nilsson, *Greek Folk Religion,* pp. 68, 78.

134. Heracles, *Nem.* VII. 86, 90, 94; Castor and Polydeuces, *Pyth.* XI. 61-62, cf. *Pyth.* V. 9-11; Semele, Ino, *Pyth.* XI. 1; Aegina, *Pyth.* VIII. 98.

135. Bowra, *Pindar,* p. 49.

136. Thompson, *The Folktale,* p. 456. Franz Boas, *Race, Language, and Culture* (New York, 1940), p. 478.

137. Paul Radin, "Literary Aspects of North American Indian Mythology," *Canada Geological Survey, Museum Bulletin,* no. 16, Anthropological Series no. 6, June 15, 1915, pp. 1-51, especially p. 28.

138. John Greenway, *Literature among the Primitives,* pp. 92-94. On p. 105 he remarks: "One would not expect to find Heracles in an Apollonian culture or Cinderella among the Dionysiacs."

139. Spencer, *Mythology and Values: An Analysis of Navaho Chantway Myths,* p. 20.

140. Radin, *The Trickster,* pp. 4-53. Greenway, *Literature among the Primitives,* pp. 84-85, 90.

141. Werner Jaeger, *Paideia,* I, 210. Heracles' prayer, *Isth.* VI. 42-49; Peleus' advice, *Il.* XI. 783; Hippolochus' advice, *Il.* VI. 207.

142. Phocus, *Nem.* V. 14-18; "hush passages," Norwood, *Pindar,* p. 80; called the *siga* motif by E. L. Bundy (*Studia Pindarica,* II, *Univ. of California Publications in Classical Philology,* vol. 18, no. 2, 1962, p. 74)—a "highlighting device whereby unpropitious matter is converted into a foil for a subsequent crescendo."

143. Achilles, *Nem.* III. 43; Peleus, *Nem.* V. 32-34; Pelops, *Ol.* I. 81-84; Chiron, *Pyth.* IX. 38 ff.; Ajax, *Nem.* VIII. 27; Polydeuces, *Nem.* X. 76-79.

144. *Pyth.* IV. 79 ff.; 102.

145. Heracles "bound by fate," *Ol.* III. 28; monsters, *Isth.* IV. 57-60; *Nem.* III. 23.

146. See above, p. 40 and note, and Farnell, II, 355, on the death of Heracles' children.

147. According to a scholiast on the passage (*Isth.* IV. 87a, p. 235. 24 Dr.) Herodorus said that Heracles was four cubits and a foot in height (approximately seven feet!). Bowra (*Pindar,* p. 48) thinks Pindar has defied tradition in his desire to please his short Theban patron; Wilamowitz (*Pindaros,* p. 340) says Heracles was small in comparison with Antaeus, though Pindar's statement is an extraordinary one; Farnell (II, 354) rejects this last suggestion, and wonders whether Pindar may be thinking of the dwarf Cretan Heracles. Rose points out (*Mythology,* p. 293) in his discussion of *Märchen* motifs that both Odysseus and Heracles were small men, at least as compared to the giants they conquered. In note 45 on this discussion he refers to *Od.* IX. 515 for Odysseus, and apparently mis-cites *Isth.* IV. 52. See Susan Feldmann, *African Myths and Tales,* pp. 14-15, for Anansi the Spider, and the African trickster.

148. Cyrene, *Pyth.* IX. 17-27; Coronis, *Pyth.* III. 25 ff.; Clytemnestra, *Pyth.* XI. 22-27.

149. Farnell, II, xiv, 223-224; Bowra, *Pindar,* p. 405.

MISCELLANEOUS MOTIFS

1. Origin of Games: Olympian, Heracles, *Ol.* II. 3; III. 21; X. 57. Nemean, Adrastus, *Nem.* X. 28. Games at Sicyon, Adrastus, *Nem.* IX. 9; *Isth.* IV. 26.

Origin of Cities: Cyrene, founded by Battus, *Pyth.* IV. 6; Thebes by Cadmus, *Pyth.* VIII. 47.

Inventions: pediments, dithyramb, bridle, *Ol.* XIII. 18-22; lyre, *Ol.* I. 17; for wryneck, *Pyth.* IV. 214, see below, p. 80.

2. Hymn to Thebes, *Fr.* 30. See Farnell, II, 390-391; Hesiod, *Theogony,* 886-900.

3. W. K. C. Guthrie, *In the Beginning* (Ithaca, 1957), p. 18.

4. *Ol.* VII. 35-38. Theia, mother of the Sun god, Helius, is invoked in *Isth.* V. 1, a passage which Farnell (I, 271-73) calls "notable" since she is a little-known goddess "who had no reality in the Greek Pantheon." Farnell praises Wilamowitz' thorough analysis and appreciation of this passage (*Pindaros,* pp. 201-202), and sums up what is apparently Pindar's conception of the goddess as a "divine potency, manifesting itself in all forms of light and brightness, in the glitter of gold, in the glory of the racing horse, and the splendour of the racing ship." Hesiod (*Theogony,* 135 and 371) merely mentions her as the

child of Uranus and Gaea, and the wife of Hyperion. (Keats, in his *Hyperion*, endows this vague "Goddess of the infant world" with pathos and beauty.) Helius, her son, is an actor in the apportionment of Rhodes (*Ol.* VII. 14, 58), while the vivid but dubiously certified *Fragment* 356 describes him as a horseman, with streaming hair, carrying a blazing torch. Moon (perhaps the same as his sister Selene) appears in *Ol.* III. 20 in a golden car.

5. Rose, *Handbook of Greek Literature*, p. 153; Farnell, II, 167. Burton (*Pindar's Pythian Odes*, p. 172) thinks *Fr.* 35—"released from these fetters by your hands, King"—may also be an allusion to the freeing of the Titans, but Farnell, in the passage just cited, is doubtful.

6. *Ol.* II. 70, 75-77; *Isth.* VIII. 32.

7. Sky Father and Earth Mother: Thompson, *The Folktale*, p. 304; Feldmann, *The Story Telling Stone*, p. 16. Primacy of water, p. 12; tales 4 and 5. See below, p. 61 and n. 18.

8. *The Story Telling Stone*, nos. 38, 39.

9. Birth of Athena, *Ol.* VII. 36 (schol. 66a and b); *Fr.* 34. Hesiod, *Theogony*, 924; *Homeric Hymn* XXVIII; Farnell, II, 52; Rose, *Mythology*, p. 108, and n. 25, p. 129.

10. "Zuni Emergence Myth," *The Story Telling Stone*, no. 1.

11. *Pyth.* I. 16-28; *Ol.* IV. 7; *Ol.* XIV. 21; *Fr.* 143; *Pae.* VI. 92.

12. *Pyth.* XI. 21; *Nem.* IV. 85; *Pyth.* IV. 44. The name Styx appears in *Pae.* VI. 155 (oath of gods?) and Xa. 4.

13. Frank Hamilton Cushing, *Zuñi Folk Tales* (New York, 1931), Introduction by J. W. Powell, pp. xii, xiii.

14. Boas, "Mythology and Folktales of the North American Indians," pp. 397-398: "On the North Pacific coast the notions regarding the universe are on the whole vague and contradictory; nevertheless visits to the sky play an important rôle in the tales. The ideas regarding a ladder leading to heaven, and journeys across the ocean to fabulous countries, also enter into the make-up of the Northwest-coast traditions. In the South, on the other hand, the notions in regard to the centre of the world, the lower world, and the four points of the compass, are of importance." See Thompson, *The Folktale*, p. 311. For the Stretching Tree, Sky-hole, and Sky-rope, see the Arapaho tale, "The Girl Enticed to the Sky," in Thompson's *Tales of the North American Indians*, no. LI.

15. So in Wimberly's *Folklore in the English and Scottish Ballads*, p. 108: "In travelling to the land of spirits or of fairies, ballad Otherworld itinerants must cross some sort of water barrier, a river or the sea. Crossing a river as a means of entering the world of spirits is a commonplace of literature, as in Homer, Vergil, and Dante, but it is a commonplace which rests ultimately, of course, upon primitive belief."

16. Atlas and Titans, *Pyth.* IV. 289-292; Giants, *Nem.* I. 67; Python, *Fr.* 55.

17. In a fragment of a *Paean* (VIIIa. 21) Hecuba, pregnant with Paris, dreams that she is to bear a hundred-handed monster, brandishing fire. Farnell, I, 315, thinks, however, it may be a description of a Fury. Walls of Tiryns, *Fr.* 169. 7.

18. Thompson, *The Folktale*, pp. 306, 315. Anita Birgitta Rooth, "The Creation Myths of the North American Indians," *Anthropos*, LII (1957), 497-508, Creation Myth: no. 2, "World Parents," and no. 5, "Struggle and Robbery." Franz Boas, "Mythology and Folk-tales of the North American Indians," p. 398: "The groups of fabulous beings that appear in each area exhibit also sharp characteristics; as the ice giants of the Iroquois and eastern Algonkin, the stupid giants of the Shoshoni and Kutenai, or the water-monsters of the South, the horned serpents of eastern America, the double-headed serpent of the coast of British Columbia, the giant thunder-bird of Vancouver Island, and the various forms of thunderers that are found among the different tribes of the continent." As an example of struggles against Sun and Moon, see "Coyote Arranges the Seasons of the Year," in *Indian Tales of North America*, ed. Tristram P. Coffin, no. 7, pp. 28-33; Apollodorus, *The Library*, ed. Sir James G. Frazer, II, "War of Earth on Heaven," pp. 318-326. See no. 6, "Olelbis," in *The Story Telling Stone*, for early struggles of the gods.

19. For Tiamat, see Webster, *From Mycenae to Homer*, pp. 84, 85. S. N. Kramer, *Sumerian Mythology* (Philadelphia, 1944), p. 13.

20. *Pyth.* I. 15-28; *Ol.* IV. 7. Similar description of Aetna in eruption, Aesch. *Pr. B.* 357-374. Bowra (*Pindar*, p. 242) thinks *Ol.* IV. 7 may be an echo of Aeschylus, if the *Pr. B.* is late in date. See Farnell, II, xiii and 109.

21. This is D 671, Transformation Flight. Rose rejects the story (*Cl. Quart*, XXIV, no. 2 [April, 1930], 107). See Farnell, II, 109, 466. Snell prints as *Fr.* 91 the disputed passage of Porphyrio. Wilamowitz (*Pindaros*, p. 324, n. 2) apparently accepts the story, though saying that it is remarkable that Pindar should have told such a story.

22. Rhodes, *Ol.* VII. 55-71; Omphalos, *Pyth.* IV. 4, 74, and *Fr.* 54 given in Strabo 9. 3. 6. See *The Story Telling Stone*, p. 46. Pillars, *Nem.* III. 21; *Ol.* III. 44; *Isth.* IV. 12.

23. Delos, *Fr.* 33 c and d; Atlas, *Pyth.* IV. 289. Four world columns, and support of sky, Thompson, *The Folktale*, p. 312. Tsimshian tale, *The Story Telling Stone*, no. 50, p. 252.

24. Note 46 on *Tales of the North American Indians*, p. 282; *The Folktale*, p. 313; Teton River, *The Story Telling Stone:* "Blackfoot Genesis," no. 7, p. 74.

25. T. T. Waterman, "The Explanatory Element in the Folk-Tales of the North-American Indians," *Journal of American Folk-Lore,* XXVII (1914), 1-54, especially pp. 14-15.

26. Raven, Tlingit tale in *The Story Telling Stone,* no. 13, p. 92; Pleiades, no. 20 (children); Coffin, *Indian Tales of North America,* no. 8 (children), no. 9 (puppies); Parker, *Australian Legendary Tales,* Maya-Mayi, The Seven Sisters, p. 105. Thompson, *The Folktale,* p. 312. Greenway, *Literature among the Primitives,* p. 49.

27. Coronis, *Pyth.* III. 25 ff. See Schol. (52b) on *Pyth.* III. 29, quoting Hesiod. Orion, *Nem.* II. 10-12: "It is reasonable that Orion should move not far from the mountain Pleiades." The handsome hunter Orion (his stature is referred to in *Isth.* IV. 49) and his pursuit of Pleione and her daughters with their change into constellations was a well-known Boeotian tale. Farnell on the passage (II, 252) says: "As belonging to an old Boeotian saga the story of Orion must have haunted Pindar's imagination, and he devoted a dithyramb to the subject, *vide* Frr.. 72-74." One of these fragments (72) refers to Orion's sojourn on the island of Chios, where he in a drunken fit attacked the wife or daughter of Oenopion. Apollodorus (I. 4. 3-4), following Pherecydes, tells of Oenopion's blinding Orion, and of his later recovery and revenge. *Fragment* 73 deals with his birth in Hyria in Boeotia; 74, with his pursuit of the Pleiades. Wilamowitz (*Pindaros,* p. 40) in a long discussion of the various stories about Orion speaks of his heroic character in Boeotia, the change that that character underwent in the Chian episodes, and frees Pindar from the suspicion of having traced his conception and name from *ourein* (Ovid, *Fasti* V. 495 ff.). See Hyginus, *Fab.* CXCV, and *Poet. Astr.* II. 34. Rose (*Mythology,* pp. 115-117) has a clear summary of the evidence for these various tales.

28. Dirce: *Isth.* VI. 74. Pindar has five references to this famous spring. No doubt he was well acquainted with the Theban story of Dirce, the jealous and cruel Queen, and the whole complex tale of her relations with Antiope and her sons Amphion and Zethus, though he chooses to disregard her gruesome death and the transformation of her blood to the spring—no doubt for aesthetic reasons (Apollod. III. 5. 5). Antiope, Amphion, and Zethus were early connected with Thebes: the sons were mentioned in the *Nekyia* of the *Odyssey* (XI. 260-265) as having built its walls. Pindar does once call Thebes the city of Zeathus (Zethus) (*Pae.* IX. 44). Amphion is not mentioned, though it would seem that the folklore touches of the rivalry between the brothers and the building of the walls to the music of Amphion's lyre (a detail not in Homer) might have appealed to him. Cadmus and the

stories connected with his founding of the city seem to have appealed more to his imagination.

29. Olives at Olympia, *Ol.* III. 23-32; Arethusa and Alpheus, *Nem.* I. 1; Petraios, *Pyth.* IV. 138.

30. Greenway, *Literature among the Primitives,* p. 45.

31. See below, p. 67.

32. See nn. 22, 23 above and Farnell, II, 193, Giants; II, 55, Rhodes; I, 326, Delos; II, 256, Pillars. *Fr.* 54 (Eagles). Schol. III, Dr., pp. 222, 101, on *Ol.* VII. 62 (Rhodes).

33. Richmond Lattimore, *The Poetry of Greek Tragedy* (Baltimore, 1958), p. 47. The Australian aborigines call such early times very appropriately "the Dreaming" (Greenway's *Literature among the Primitives,* p. 42).

34. Gaea, mother of gods and men, *Nem.* VI. 1-2; Erichthonius, *Fr.* 253; Erechtheus, *Pyth.* VII. 10; his descendants, *Isth.* II. 19.

35. W. R. Halliday, *Indo-European Folk-Tales and Greek Legend,* p. 9; Farnell, II, 70.

36. Ovid, *Metamorphoses* I. 414-415. See Apollod. I. 7. 2 and Grant, *The Myths of Hyginus, Fab.* CLIII and notes.

37. Thompson, *The Folktale,* pp. 305, 308; *The Story Telling Stone,* p. 17, and tale no. 7, "The Blackfoot Genesis." See Anita Birgitta Rooth, "The Creation Myths of the North American Indians," pp. 497-508, for eight different types of creation myths: Earth-Diver, World Parents (this resembles the Greek Heaven and Earth type), Emergence Myth, Spider as Creator, Struggle and Robbery, Ymir Type, Two Creators, Blind Brother.

38. Hephaestus, following Zeus' instructions, fashions Pandora from earth and water in Hesiod, *Works and Days* 60-69; Prometheus appears as man's benefactor, not his creator, in Hesiod. Rose, however, gives the evidence for an ancient popular tradition, preserved in Pausanias and some minor writers, that he actually was the creator (*Greek Mythology,* p. 54). See Hyginus, *Fab.* CXLII.

39. A possible reference to the Orphic belief that men were born from the ashes of the slain Titans Rose derives from a much-disputed passage in Pindar, *Fr.* 133, containing the words "ancient grief or woe" for which Persephone is to exact the penalty. In an article entitled "The Grief of Persephone," *Harvard Theological Review,* XXXVI (1943), 247 ff., he expressed his strong conviction that the goddess' grief was for her slain son Zagreus whom the Titans murdered. From their ashes men sprang, according to Orphic belief, and thus have in them a mixture of evil and good, partaking of both Titanic and Dionysiac elements. He had proposed this theory in an earlier article, "The Ancient Grief," *Greek Poetry and Life* (Oxford, 1936), p. 79, which was criticized

by Ivan Linforth, *The Arts of Orpheus* (Berkeley, 1941), pp. 345 ff. See also W. C. Greene, *Moira*, pp. 55, 59. Dodds, *The Greeks and the Irrational*, pp. 155 ff., with n. 131, supports Rose's view.

40. Sparti, *Pyth.* IX. 82; *Isth.* I. 30 and VII. 10. In *Fr.* 29, Hymn for the Thebans, he enumerates the subjects he would be glad to treat (this was the passage said to have aroused the criticism of Corinna), and mentions "Cadmus and the holy race of Sown-Men," Melia, Thebe, and Harmonia—all connected with the early history of Thebes. Thebe married Zethus, and the Cadmeia in her honor was renamed Thebes; Melia bore to Apollo at Thebes two sons, Ismenius and Tenerus, the latter of whom Pindar often mentions. The wedding of Cadmus and Harmonia was a favorite subject with Pindar. Niobe, wife of Amphion, does not appear in the extant writings of Pindar, though the works of the fifth-century dramatists are full of references to her.

41. Men from Teeth, *Motif-Index*, A 1265. Farnell, I, 113. Burton (*Pindar's Pythian Odes*, p. 166) gives the teeth to the wrong dragon; the teeth-sowing incident came earlier in the story, and the teeth were some of those from the dragon Cadmus had slain at Thebes.

42. Burton, *Pindar's Pythian Odes*, p. 26.

43. W. R. Halliday, *Indo-European Folk-Tales and Greek Legend*, p. 70.

44. *Ol.* VII. 39-49; Farnell, I, 38-39. Archemorus, *Bacchylides* 56 (J. M. Edmonds, *Lyra Graeca* [London, 1922-1927]).

45. See Farnell, II, Excursus, 459-476, for an enlightening discussion of Pindar's religious views. Hera, *Pyth.* IV. 184; Hermes, *Pyth.* IX. 59; Aphrodite, *Pyth.* IX. 9; Artemis, *Ol.* III. 26.

46. Zeus, *Isth.* VII. 5-7; Triton? *Pyth.* IV. 33; Apollo, *Pyth.* III. 43; Gods, *Ol.* VII. 55 ff.; *Isth.* VIII. 26; *Pae.* VI. 75-95.

47. Richmond Lattimore, *The Poetry of Greek Tragedy*, p. 21 and note 10.

48. *Ibid.*, p. 47, n. 24.

49. Theft from the Sun, *The Story Telling Stone*, no. 25, p. 149; Star Husband, Tristram P. Coffin, *Indian Tales of North America*, no. 22, p. 89. Dawn Boy, *The Primitive Reader*, edited by John Greenway, pp. 28-31.

50. The marriage of Peleus and Thetis here and in *Nem.* IV. 65 ff., and V. 23 ff. The marriage of Cadmus and Harmonia, closely associated with the legendary history of Thebes, was early famous; Apollodorus quotes Pherecydes in his account of it (III. 4. 2). It is mentioned in the "Corinna fragment," one of the earliest compositions of Pindar (29), and also in *Dith.* II. 27-30. Diodorus, in a passage (V. 48-49) which Wilamowitz (*Pindaros*, p. 38) thinks may contain some Pindaric material, says it was the first mortal marriage attended by the gods, and

enumerates the gifts—the famous necklace, a robe, and musical instruments. Apollo played upon the lyre, the Muses upon their flutes, and all the gods helped in the celebration of the wedding. The happy mortal bridegrooms are mentioned in the Blessed Islands of *Olympian* II. Farnell comments on Pindar's interest in these weddings (II, 142).

51. *The Story Telling Stone*, no. 3, "The Monster Slayers"; no. 39, "The Girl Enticed to the Sky"; no. 33, "The Man Who Acted as Sun"; and Introduction, pp. 32-33. For similar tabus of eating and drinking in the Otherworld in English and Scottish ballads, see L. C. Wimberly, *Folklore in the English and Scottish Ballads*, pp. 275-282.

52. Tantalus, *Ol.* I. 60-64; Asclepius, *Pyth.* III. 55-57. With regard to Asclepius, Lattimore, in *The Poetry of Greek Tragedy* (p. 47, n. 24), has made an interesting suggestion. In referring to this passage of Pindar (comparing also *Agamemnon*, 1017-24, and *Alcestis*, 122-31) he says: "The unstated inference from his story seems to be that only since the blasting of Asclepius has the law held good that the dead must stay dead forever." One could draw parallels with several Indian tales, such as the Cherokee Orpheus (Thompson, *Tales*, LV, p. 147): "If the men had kept the box closed, as the Little Men told them to do, they would have brought her home safely, and we could bring back our other friends also from the Ghost country, but now when they die we can never bring them back." The inevitability of death seems to have been brought about by this single specific act.

53. Tityus, *Pyth.* IV. 90-92; Ixion, *Pyth.* II. 35-39; Bellerophon, *Isth.* VII. 44-46.

54. Otus and Ephialtes, *Frr.* 162, 163. The presumptuous deed of these giants is told as early as *Odyssey* XI. 308 ff. Pindar simply places their death in Naxos, but the scholiast on the passage (Drachmann, II, 156a, p. 121.7), as well as Apollodorus (I. 7. 4), tells how Artemis sent a deer between them, and in their eagerness to kill it, they slew one another. *Fr.* 163 of Pindar, "Fixing mutually murdering spears in each other," could imply this story. See Grant, *Myths of Hyginus*, XXVIII, and the note there on the trick of diverting the attention of fighting men to bring about mutual slaughter.

55. Susan Feldmann, *African Myths and Tales*, no. 8, The Tower to Heaven; no. 108, The Old Woman Who Tried to Find God.

56. Salmoneus, *Pyth.* IV. 143; Semele, *Ol.* II. 25-26; *Pyth.* XI. 1; Farnell, II, 469.

57. Theodor H. Gaster, in commenting on Frazer's treatment of tabu (in *The New Golden Bough*, p. 265), says: "Taboo is not always, as he [Frazer] supposes, a formal ritual or social prohibition . . . and a careful distinction must be made between taboos and avoidances. There are many things which people avoid (e.g., going near fire) not

out of a sense of awe or 'numinosity' but simply out of caution born of experience. It might be useful, for purely practical classification, to distinguish between taboos imposed for the benefit of the subject and those imposed for the benefit of the object." The tabus in the Greek examples all seem to be Gaster's second type.

58. *The Story Telling Stone,* no. 35, "The Man Who Brought His Wife Back From Spirit Land"; no. 36, "Coyote and Eagle Visit the Land of the Dead." In this latter tale, spirits in ceremonial robes beautifully decorated with shells and elks' teeth, were dancing and singing in a large lodge bright with moonlight. The ashes that must be thrown behind to delay the hostile pursuing spirits in the first tale, and the whish of wind when the partially revived dead escape from Coyote's basket on his return trip furnish eerie notes that recall the atmosphere of the *Nekyia* of the *Odyssey.* See also Mrs. Feldmann's Introduction, p. 33.

59. Angelia, *Ol.* VIII. 77-82. See Wilamowitz (*Pindaros,* p. 39) on Pindar's rivid personifications. Farnell (II, 66) points out that Angelia is an original personification found nowhere else in Greek literature, suitably called the daughter of Hermes, the "Conductor of Souls." Hermes does not appear in the odes performing this function. Echo, another of Pindar's personifications, appears in *Ol.* XIV. 20. See also *Nem.* IV. 85 for a third example showing the sentiency of the dead. Bowra's statement (*Pindar,* p. 95, n. 2) that Pindar had the Homeric conception of survival after death is incomplete in this respect. There is in Pindar no suggestion of the necessary drinking of blood as in Homer, and the dead seem like normal human beings.

60. Coronis, *Pyth.* III. 11; Archilochus, *Fr.* 55 D; Farnell, I, 286, thinks Pindar's reference in *Isth.* VIII. 10 is to the fear that disgraced Thebes might lose her autonomy after her punishment by the Greek army; Tantalus, *Ol.* I. 57. See Farnell, II, 8, for three other sinners; Bowra, *Pindar,* p. 79, for three other kinds of punishment. Wilamowitz (*Pindaros,* p. 236, n. 4) says the passage is unclear, but in any case Tantalus has eternal punishment. On p. 288 he compares Ixion with Tantalus; both have lived with the gods and partaken of the food of the gods; therefore, immortality makes punishment everlasting. Both stories, he concludes, are older than the idea of a common realm of the dead. Cf. Bowra, *Pindar,* p. 79: Tantalus "may even suffer his doom on Olympus." Norwood, *Pindar,* n. 49 on p. 216, says that in 1873 Comparetti proved that the scene is *not* in Hades. Comparetti states that the stone hangs over Tantalus at the banquet of he gods, as in Athen. 281 B, and that scholars have been misled by *Odyssey* XI. 583 ff., where the stone is not mentioned. Lord Raglan ("Myth and Ritual," in *Myth, A Symposium,* ed. Thomas A. Sebeok [Bloomington,

1958], p. 78) in support of his theory of ritual origin of many myths quotes the classicist Halliday on the Tantalus story: "The story of the serving up of Pelops by Tantalus may . . . have had a ritual origin and have been in the first place connected with some rite of human sacrifice and sacrament." See Halliday, *Indo-European Folk-Tales and Greek Legend*, pp. 69-70, for his considered view on the whole question of the interaction of myth and ritual. See above, nn. 42 and 43.

61. Dirges, *Frr.* 129, 130, 131, 133. See Greene, *Moira*, pp. 78-81.

62. Tower of Cronus, Farnell, II, 19.

63. Achilles, *Ol.* II. 79-80; in other places *(Nem.* VIII. 30, *Isth.* VIII. 57), Achilles' death is referred to.

64. Pelops and Ganymede, *Ol.* I. 41, 44; Castor and Polydeuces, *Nem.* X. 55, 87-88; Aristaeus, *Pyth.* IX. 60-64.

65. Pindar may have written about Glaucus. See *Fr.* 263 with the source, Paus. IX. 22. 7; Erwin Rohde *(Psyche* [New York, 1925], chap. II, pp. 55-87) lists a few "translations" from mortality to godhood in Homer, Hesiod, and the Epic Cycle. Mimnermus *(Fr.* 4 Diehl) says Zeus gave an evil—"imperishable old age"—to Tithonus. According to the *Motif-Index* immortality may be forfeited by the breaking of some tabu (C 937.1).

66. Rohde, *Psyche,* chap. III, p. 90.

67. Trophonius, *Fr.* 2. 3 (reference here is only to the death in sleep of Agamedes and Trophonius, who were said to have built the fourth temple of Apollo at Delphi; but Pindar may have told more of their story and the shrine in this lost *Isthmian* Ode). See Bowra, *Pindar*, p. 375; Puech, IV, 87; Amphiaraus, *Ol.* VI. 13-14; *Nem.* IX. 24-25; *Nem.* X. 8-9; oracle, *Pyth.* VIII. 39-55.

68. Caeneus, *Fr.* 167 *(Dirges* VI).

69. See Rohde, n. 3, pp. 103-104.

70. Halliday *(Indo-European Folk-Tales and Greek Legend,* p. 72) in referring to the Meleager story calls the invocation of the underworld powers by beating on the ground "a very ancient piece of ritual." Another example occurs in the *Homeric Hymn to Pythian Apollo*, III. 333, where Hera strikes the ground with her flattened hand and prays to Earth and the Titan gods dwelling beneath the earth that she may conceive and bear a child apart from Zeus. See also *The Story Telling Stone,* no. 44, The Two Sisters.

71. Joseph Campbell, *The Masks of God: Primitive Mythology,* pp. 173-176. C. H. Long, *Alpha, The Myths of Creation* (New York, 1963), p. 224. A dramatic tale of a maiden devoted to sacrifice to bring rain may be found in Feldmann's *African Myths and Tales,* no. 97, The Maiden who was Sacrificed by her Kin. She stood in the middle of a circle of her kinsmen and began to sink into the ground, crying out,

"I am lost, but much rain will come." She gradually disappeared, the earth closed over her and the rain came down in torrents. Her grieving lover came to the spot where she sank, and himself began to sink. He went by a "long road under the earth" to find her and bring her back. Finally they both rose to the air.

72. *Met.* XII. 525. A similar story of the soul escaping as a bird in *The Story Telling Stone,* no. 34. See L. C. Wimberly, *Folklore in the English and Scottish Ballads,* pp. 44-52.

73. Hyginus, *Fab.* CCXLII. Rose thinks the passage corrupt; it differs from all other accounts; but, in a sense, it *was* a suicide. For Caeneus, see Heckenbach's article "Kaineus" in Pauly-Wissowa.

74. Euxantius, *Pae.* IV. 35-45. Wilamowitz edited the fragment minutely (*Pindaros,* pp. 471-477). Farnell says of it (I, 304): "Nothing was known about him (Euxantius) until the discovery of Bacchylides' *Odes* and Pindar's *Paean.* Bacchylides calls Ceos 'island of Euxantios.' Pindar may have based his picturesque narrative on an antiquarian pretension of the islanders that they still possessed the family house of Euxantius and on the tradition of an earthquake that destroyed the rest of the island." Dexithea, mother of Euxantius, appears in Bacchylides' ode in honor of Argeius of Ceos (29). Damon, Macelo, and the wizard Telchines are others connected with the family in little-known tales. See Edmonds, *Lyra Graeca,* III, 127. Bowra (*Pindar,* pp. 364-65) comments on the use of the first person in Pindar's narrative.

75. Pelops, *Ol.* I. 37-64. For the usual version of the story of Tantalus and Pelops see Hyginus, *Fabulae* LXXXII and LXXXIII (with Rose's comments and my own) in *The Myths of Hyginus,* pp. 76-77. The scholiast on *Ol.* I. 37 (Drachmann, I, 30b, 40a) refers to a treatment of the theme by Bacchylides, who stated that Rhea instead of Zeus restored Pelops by putting him back again into the caldron. The story has the air of genuine folklore (see Thompson, *The Folktale,* p. 255, on various means of resuscitation). An Indian parallel for the assembling of members for resuscitation may be seen in "The Sun Tests his Son-In-Law," no. XXXIX of Thompson's *Tales of the North American Indians,* p. 79, which gives the special feature of the story that one missing member causes deformity in the revived animal or person. The little girl is at first blind, and the boy lame. So Pelops in the usual version of the story must be provided with an ivory shoulder. Farnell, II, 6.

76. Iolaus, *Pyth.* IX. 79. Aphrodite gives Ganymede the bloom of eternal youth (*Ol.* X. 104-105).

77. Farnell, II, 148, 159.

131

78. Amphiaraus, *Pyth.* VIII. 39-55; children of Heracles, *Isth.* IV. 61-68; Farnell, II, 355.

79. "Cloud Hera" and wheel, *Pyth.* II. 36-41; Lord Raglan ("Myth and Ritual," in T. A. Sebeok, *Myth, A Symposium,* p. 78), seeking support for his theory of ritual origin from classical scholars, quotes A. B. Cook, *Zeus,* I, 211, 218, who refers the legend of Ixion to a ritual in which a man was bound to a wheel and sacrificed in the character of the sun god. Cf. Frazer's edition of Apollodorus, II. 148. See Theodor H. Gaster (*The New Golden Bough*), on fire-wheels or discs at fire festivals, pp. 699, 700, 711, 728, 730, 731. Robert Graves, *The Greek Myths,* I, 209.

80. *Pyth.* IV. 214-217; *Nem.* IV. 35.

81. J. H. Finley, Jr., *Pindar and Aeschylus,* p. 94.

82. Farnell, II, 124.

83. Stesichorus, 18 (*Lyra Graeca,* ed. J. M. Edmonds, II, 45). See Frazer's note on Apollodorus, *Ep.* III. 3-5.

84. Lattimore, *The Poetry of Greek Tragedy,* pp. 122-125.

85. Susan Feldmann, *The Story Telling Stone,* p. 32. Compare "Walking Skeleton" in *Indian Tales of North America,* ed. Tristram P. Coffin, p. 51.

86. Catherine H. Berndt, "The Ghost Husband," pp. 244-277, esp. p. 252, in *The Anthropologist Looks at Myth.*

87. Animal Wives and Husbands in American Indian tales, Thompson, *The Folktale,* pp. 353 ff.; for examples, Thompson, *Tales of the North American Indians,* chap. VI, pp. 150-173. Bowra, *Pindar,* p. 295, for Centaurus. Hyginus, *Fab.* LXII, for usual parentage of Centaurs. P. Grimal in his *Dictionnaire de la Mythologie Grecque et Romaine,* "Nephele," discusses the conception of the Clouds in Aristophanes' play and thinks there may be Orphic influence or influence of vague folklore beliefs there.

88. Werner Jaeger, *Paideia,* I, 206.

89. Tantalus and Pelops, *Ol.* I. 36-52. Farnell comments (I, 8): Pindar seeks to "amend the traditional version by substituting the motive of a divine amour for a cannibalistic sacrifice." Wilamowitz (*Pindaros,* p. 236) deplores in such substitution the union of pious feeling with customs our age shrinks from.

90. *Fr.* 283; *Motif-Index,* D 1413. 6, magic seat which holds one fast.

91. Farnell, II, 463.

92. *Pae.* VI. 75-86.

93. *Frr.* 2 and 3 (the latter from Plutarch, *Consol. Apoll.* 14, p. 109 A). Two other myths of deception by the gods may underlie troublesome lines in *Isth.* VIII: one (lines 57, 58 arranged by Farnell; 46a, 47 by Snell), the story that Thetis concealed Achilles in Scyros as a girl to

keep him safe, the other (line 59 according to Farnell; 50 according to Snell) that the god Dionysus entangled Telephus in a vine in Mysia, so that he fell before Achilles. The adjective "vine-clad" for Mysia here seems to suggest this story. See Farnell, I, 287, and II, 382-383. Norman O. Brown in his *Hermes the Thief* (Madison, 1947), chap. I, draws the distinction between cattle-raiding (robbery—Heracles the representative) and thievery (showing mental skill and cunning—Hermes the representative). In the *Homeric Hymn to Hermes*, despite the cattle-lifting, stealth and magical power are stressed. Brown concludes (p. 19) that an "analysis of the oldest stratum of Greek mythology reveals that behind Hermes the Thief is Hermes the Trickster, and behind Hermes the Trickster is Hermes the Magician."

94. *The Folktale,* p. 138.

95. *Iliad* XIX. 407.

96. Paus. X. 24. 5.

97. Themis, *Isth.* VIII. 31; Fates, *Ol.* VII. 64; Chiron, *Pyth.* IX. 51 ff.; Tiresias, *Nem.* I. 61; *Isth.* VII. 8; Tenerus (an obscure local prophet, though a great favorite with Pindar), *Fr.* 51d, *Pae.* VII. 13, IX. 41; Iamus, *Ol.* VI. 50, 65-66; Polyidus, *Ol.* XIII. 74 ff.; Melampus, *Pae.* IV. 28; Mopsus, *Pyth.* IV. 191; Cassandra, *Pyth.* XI. 33; *Pae.* VIIIa. 9; Medea, *Pyth.* IV. 10 ff.; Heracles, *Isth.* VI. 51-54.

98. Ismenian temple, *Pyth.* XI. 6; Amphiaraus, *Ol.* VI. 16; *Pyth.* VIII. 39; pyromancy, *Ol.* VIII. 3; flight of birds, *Pyth.* IV. 191; thunder, *Pyth.* IV. 197; nod of gods, *Nem.* I. 14; *Isth.* VIII. 46; dreams, *Ol.* XIII. 66, 79; *Pyth.* IV. 163; *Pae.* VIIIa. 17. The six Enchantresses (Celedones) who "sang above the eagle" on the third temple of Apollo at Delphi (*Pae.* VIII. 70, 71) must have been prophetic Sirens of a sort. See Bowra, *Pindar,* pp. 373-75; Aimé Puech, *Pindare* (Paris, 1961), IV, 134-136; and Walter Miller, *Daedalus and Thespis* (New York, 1929), I, 51-52.

99. Thompson, *The Folktale,* pp. 139, 267; Themis, *Isth.* VIII. 32-33.

100. Thompson, *The Folktale,* p. 141; oracle to Pelias, *Pyth.* IV. 75; oracle to Pelias to escort spirit of Phrixus home, *Pyth.* IV. 163-164; Amphiaraus, *Pyth.* VIII. 46.

101. Decree of gods or fate, *Pae.* VI. 92-95; *Fr.* 140a. 66-68; arrows of Heracles, *Pyth.* I. 55; Hecuba's dream and Cassandra's prophecy, *Pae.* VIIIa. 10-23. The conjecture of Sitzler for line 25—her forethought "failed"—might indicate knowledge of the detail that her prophecies were not to be believed.

102. Neoptolemus, *Nem.* VII. 44 ff.; *Pae.* VI. 112 ff.

103. Division M, Ordaining the Future, does not appear in Thompson's special index for his *Tales of the North American Indians.* An instance appears in the tale W. A. Lessa entitles "Discoverer-of-the-Sun"

(*The Anthropologist Looks at Myth,* p. 38), in which a man covered with yaws warns the people that they are threatening the son of Iolofath, a god, but his warning is ignored. Again, a blind canoe-builder, really a god in disguise, gives a futile warning. Lessa concludes: "The two above-mentioned gods, who have the power of near-omniscience, do not interfere because intervention would spoil the bold events in store for the listeners. We have something approximating the inexorable denouements that the Greeks loved so well."

104. Phocus, *Nem.* V. 14; Heracles, *Isth.* IV. 63 ff., and Farnell, II, 355.

105. Diomede, *Nem.* X. 7 (12b); Farnell, II, 318. If the child Achilles (*Nem.* III. 48) brings to Chiron the "still-panting" bodies of the beasts he has slain (Pindar is the first literary authority for this picture of the boy's prowess in hunting), he may be seeking in a similar way to acquire their "mana," but the possible significance of Pindar's phrase is not pressed. Farnell, II, 258; Bowra, *Pindar,* p. 287.

106. *Pyth.* XI. 22, Iphigenia; XI. 20, Cassandra; *Nem.* X. 6, Hypermnestra.

107. *Pae.* V. 42; Farnell, II, 400. She was changed to a quail before her leap into the sea, according to Apollod. I. 4. 1; hence the connection of the name Ortygia (Quail land) and Delos.

108. *Ol.* III. 30 (53c, d).

109. Apollod. I. 9. 3; III. 12. 6; Halliday, *Greek and Roman Folklore,* p. 94; change to stone, Scholiast on *Iliad* I. 180; *Isth.* VIII. 21; *Nem.* VII. 50; *Nem.* VIII. 6.

110. Rhoecus, *Frr.* 165 and 252.

111. This statement holds true in spite of Pindar's frequent "circular pattern" of composition, that is, "anticipating the crisis, and then telling how it comes about." Bowra, *Pindar,* p. 310. The story of Coronis furnishes a good example: The poet thinks of Chiron, nurse of Asclepius, the kindly physician, whose mother Coronis, before his birth, was slain by Artemis and angry Apollo. Then comes the story explaining her death—her infidelity to Apollo through infatuation with a mortal, Apollo's detection of this love, his decision to punish her, and his rescue of the unborn child on the funeral pyre. Chiron's tendance of Asclepius is mentioned again, to be followed by the account of the young physician's wonderful cures, his presumption in restoring a man to life, and his punishment by Zeus.

112. *Greek and Roman Folklore,* p. 80.

113. *The Folktale,* p. 279.

114. *Greek and Roman Folklore,* p. 92.

115. *The Folktale,* pp. 279, 280.

116. *Greek and Roman Folklore,* p. 94.

117. *Nem.* IV. 54-61; *Nem.* V. 25-37.

118. Frazer's note 4 on Apollod. III. 13. 3. W. Mannhardt, *Antike Wald und Feldkulte* (Berlin, 1877), pp. 49 ff. A. Lesky, in the article "Peleus-Thetis" in Pauly-Wissowa (especially pp. 284-286), brings out the *Märchen* elements in the story—the unhappiness of the sea-bride won by wrestling, the "speechless marriage" referred to by the scholiast on *Nem.* III. 35 (60) quoting Sophocles' *Troilus, Fr.* 561, the departure of the offended bride because of her husband's condemnation of her attempts to gain supernatural qualities for her children, and the consequent rearing of Achilles by another. The scholiast terms the story "popular."

119. Hesiod in Schol. on Pindar, *Nem.* IV. 59 (95b). See again Apollod. III. 13. 3 and Frazer's long note, also his note 1 on the "tongue episode."

120. Peleus' spear, *Nem.* III. 33-34; *Nem.* IV. 54, Iolcus.

121. Motifs omitted: attempts to make child immortal, abandonment by offended fairy bride, silence of bride.

122. Nilsson, *Greek Folk Religion,* p. 12; see also Lawson, *Modern Greek Folklore and Ancient Greek Religion,* pp. 252, 253.

123. *Fr.* 166, Pheres (Centaurs) drunk; *Dirges* VI, Caeneus, Battle with Lapiths; "Divine beast," *Pyth.* IV. 119; *Pyth.* III. 1-8, 63-67; *Nem.* III. 54-55.

124. Schol. on Ap. Rhod. I. 554, and II. 1231, quoting Pherecydes.

125. Frazer on Apollod. III. 6. 7, n. 1.

126. *Pyth.* IV. 102-105, Jason; *Nem.* III. 43, Achilles; *Pyth.* III. 1-7, Asclepius; *Nem.* III. 52-54, Jason and Asclepius. Hesiod had described Chiron as educating Medeus (*Theog.* 1001) and Jason and Achilles (Scholiast on Homer, *Od.* XII. 69, and *Catalogues of Women,* p. 198, ed. Evelyn-White), but Farnell (II, 258) says he appears for the first time in literature in Pindar as rearing Achilles in his cave. Chiron as prophet, *Pyth.* IX. 38-66.

127. Thompson, *The Folktale,* pp. 384 ff. *The Story Telling Stone,* p. 11, and Tale no. 19: "The Twins Alter the Book of Life," p. 102. Thompson, *Tales of the North American Indians,* V, "The Woman Who Fell from the Sky," p. 14.

128. Farnell, II, 322. Though Farnell first thought the details Pindar used in this narrative were all derived from the *Cypria,* he changed his mind later.

129. Farnell, II, 322-23. Apollod. III. 11. 2.

130. *Motif-Index,* R 311 ff.

131. Lynceus, *Motif-Index,* F 642. 3. 1.

132. Halliday, *Greek and Roman Folklore,* p. 57, referring to tombstones as "the things which must not be moved," and giving Hesiod,

Works and Days, 750, as a reference. Apollodorus speaks only of a stone as a weapon, but Hyginus, *Fab.* LXXX, expressly states it was a funeral monument. Wilamowitz (*Pindaros,* p. 428) calls this tale Pindar's finest narrative, and Farnell (1, 230) characterizes the end of the ode as "swift, strong, terse, and thrilling."

Summary

1. *The Folktale,* pp. 278-281.
2. *Pyth.* IV. 247-250.
3. Schol. II Dr. 195 ff.
4. Bowra, *Pindar,* p. 283, and W. C. Wright, *Short History of Greek Literature,* p. 129, "anti-Homeric bias."
5. Wilamowitz, *Pindaros,* pp. 37-42.
6. Bowra, *Pindar,* p. 285.
7. Pausanias IX. 22. 7.
8. Farnell, II, 472, 466.
9. Bowra, *Pindar,* pp. 381 ff.
10. Bowra, *Pindar,* p. 380.
11. Epithets, Bowra, *Pindar,* pp. 43, 214-216.
12. Schol. II Dr. 370.
13. Quintilian, *Inst. Or.* X. 1. 63.
14. Bowra, *Pindar,* pp. 322, 354, 358.
15. Burton, *Pindar's Pythian Odes,* p. 124.
16. Schol. I Dr. 157a.
17. Farnell, II, 163.

Bibliography

Berndt, Catherine H. "The Ghost Husband," in *The Anthropologist Looks at Myth*, compiled by Melville Jacobs, edited by John Greenway. Austin: Univ. of Texas Press, 1966.

Boas, Franz. "Mythology and Folktales of the North American Indians," *Journal of American Folklore*, XXVII (1914), 374-410.

———. *Race, Language, and Culture*. New York: Macmillan, 1940.

Bolte, Johannes, and Georg Polívka. *Anmerkungen zu den Kinder und Hausmärchen der Brüder Grimm*. Leipzig, 1913-32.

Bolton, J. D. P. *Aristeas of Proconnesus*. Oxford: Clarendon Press, 1962.

Bowra, C. M. *Pindari Carmina* (2nd ed.). London: Oxford Univ. Press, 1952.

———. *Heroic Poetry*. London: Macmillan, 1952.

———. *The Greek Experience*. Cleveland: World Publishing Co., 1957.

———. *Pindar*. Oxford: Clarendon Press, 1964.

Brown, Norman O. *Hermes the Thief*. Madison: Univ. of Wisconsin Press, 1947.

Bundy, Elroy L. *Studia Pindarica*. 2 vols. Berkeley: Univ. of California Press, 1962.

Burn, A. R. *The Lyric Age of Greece*. New York: St. Martin's Press, 1960.

Burton, R. W. B. *Pindar's Pythian Odes*. London: Oxford Univ. Press, 1962.

Bury, J. B. *The Nemean Odes of Pindar*. London: Macmillan, 1890.

———. *The Isthmian Odes of Pindar*. London: Macmillan, 1892.

Campbell, Joseph. *The Hero with a Thousand Faces*. ("Bollingen Series," XVII.) New York: Pantheon Books, 1949.

———. *The Masks of God: Primitive Mythology*. New York: Viking Press, 1959.

Carpenter, Rhys. *Folktale, Fiction, and Saga in the Homeric Epics*. Berkeley: Univ. of California Press, 1962.

Chadwick, H. M. and N. K. Chadwick. *The Growth of*

Literature. 3 vols. Cambridge: Cambridge Univ. Press, 1932-40.

Clodd, Edward. *Magic in Names and in Other Things.* London: Chapman and Hall, Ltd., 1920.

Coffin, Tristram P. *Indian Tales of North America.* ("Bibliographical and Special Series," XIII.) Philadelphia: American Folklore Society, Inc., 1961.

Croiset, Alfred. *La Poésie de Pindare* (2nd ed.). Paris, 1886.

Cushing, Frank Hamilton. *Zuñi Folk-tales.* Introduction by J. W. Powell. New York: Knopf, 1931.

De Vries, Jan. *Heroic Song and Heroic Legend.* Translated by B. J. Timmer. London: Oxford Univ. Press, 1963.

Dodds, E. R. *Euripides' Bacchae.* Oxford: Clarendon Press, 1944.

———. *The Greeks and the Irrational.* (Sather Classical Lectures, XXV.) Berkeley: Univ. of California Press, 1951.

Drachmann, A. B. *Scholia Vetera in Pindari Carmina.* Leipzig: Teubner, 1927.

Dundes, Alan. *The Study of Folklore.* Englewood Cliffs, New Jersey: Prentice-Hall, Inc., 1965.

Edmonds, J. M. *Lyra Graeca.* 3 vols. London: Wm. Heinemann, 1922-27.

Farnell, Lewis Richard. *The Works of Pindar.* Translated with Literary and Critical Commentaries. 2 vols. London: Macmillan and Co., 1930 and 1932. (Vol. II, *Critical Commentary to the Works of Pindar,* reprinted, Amsterdam: A. M. Hakkert, 1961.)

Feldmann, Susan (ed.). *African Myths and Tales.* New York: Dell (Laurel Edition), 1963.

———. *The Story Telling Stone, Myths and Tales of the American Indians.* New York: Dell (Laurel Edition), 1965.

Fennell, C. A. M. *Pindar: The Nemean and Isthmian Odes.* Cambridge: Cambridge Univ. Press, 1883.

———. *Pindar: The Olympian and Pythian Odes.* Cambridge: Cambridge Univ. Press, 1893.

Finley, J. H., Jr. *Pindar and Aeschylus.* (Martin Classical Lectures, XIV.) Cambridge: Published for Oberlin College by Harvard Univ. Press, 1955.

Fox, W. S. *Greek and Roman Mythology.* Boston: Marshall Jones Company, 1916.

Frazer, Sir J. G. (ed. and tr.). Apollodorus, *The Library*. 2 vols. London: Wm. Heinemann, 1921.

———. *The Golden Bough*. See Gaster, Theodor H.

Gaster, Theodor H. *The Oldest Stories in the World*. New York: Viking, 1952.

———. *The New Golden Bough*. Edited with Notes and Foreword. New York: Mentor Book, New American Library, 1964.

Gildersleeve, Basil L. *Pindar: The Olympian and Pythian Odes* (2nd ed.). New York, 1890.

Grant, Mary A. *The Myths of Hyginus*. Lawrence: Univ. of Kansas Press, 1960.

Graves, Robert. *The Greek Myths*. 2 vols. Baltimore: Penguin Books, 1955.

Greene, W. C. *Moira: Fate, Good, and Evil in Greek Thought*. Cambridge: Harvard Univ. Press, 1944 (Harper Torchbook, 1963).

Greenway, John. *Literature among the Primitives*. Hatboro, Pa.: Folklore Associates, 1964.

——— (ed.). *The Primitive Reader*. Hatboro, Pa.: Folklore Associates, 1965.

Grimal, Pierre. *Dictionnaire de la mythologie Grecque et Romaine*. Paris: Presses Universitaires de France, 1958.

Guthrie, W. K. C. *The Greeks and Their Gods*. Boston: Beacon Press, 1951.

———. *In the Beginning*. Ithaca: Cornell Univ. Press, 1957.

Halliday, W. R. *Greek and Roman Folklore*. New York: Longmans, Green and Co., 1927.

———. *Indo-European Folk-Tales and Greek Legend*. Cambridge: Cambridge Univ. Press, 1933.

Hartland, E. S. *The Legend of Perseus*. 3 vols. London, 1894-96.

Herskovits, Melville. *Man and His Works*. New York: Knopf, 1948.

Herskovits, Melville J. and Frances S. Herskovits. *Dahomean Narrative*. Evanston, Ill.: Northwestern Univ. Press, 1958.

Jacobs, Melville, and John Greenway. *The Anthropologist Looks at Myth*. Austin: Univ. of Texas Press, for the American Folklore Society, 1966.

Jaeger, Werner. *Paideia*. 3 vols. New York: Oxford Univ. Press, 1943-45.

Jebb, Sir Richard. *Bacchylides.* Cambridge: Cambridge Univ. Press, 1905.

Klapp, Orrin E. "The Folk Hero," *Journal of American Folklore,* LXII (1949), 17-25.

Kramer, S. N. *Sumerian Mythology.* Philadelphia: American Philosophical Society, 1944 (Harper Torchbook, 1961).

Krappe, Alexander H. *The Science of Folklore.* New York: Barnes and Noble, 1930.

Lattimore, Richmond (tr.). *The Odes of Pindar.* Chicago: Univ. of Chicago Press, 1947.

———. *The Poetry of Greek Tragedy.* Baltimore: Johns Hopkins Press, 1958.

Lawson, John Cuthbert. *Modern Greek Folklore and Ancient Greek Religion.* Cambridge: Cambridge Univ. Press, 1910.

Long, Charles H. *Alpha: The Myths of Creation.* New York: George Braziller, 1963.

Lowie, Robert H. "The Test Theme in North American Mythology," *Journal of American Folklore,* XXI (1908), 97-148.

Mannhardt, W. *Antike Wald und Feldkulte.* Berlin, 1877.

Miller, Walter. *Daedalus and Thespis.* New York: Macmillan, 1929.

Murray, Gilbert. *Rise of the Greek Epic* (3rd ed.). Oxford: Clarendon Press, 1924.

Murray, Henry A. (ed.). *Myth and Mythmaking.* New York: Braziller, 1960.

Nilsson, Martin P. *Greek Folk Religion* (first published as *Greek Popular Religion.* New York: Columbia Univ. Press, 1940). New York: Harper and Brothers, 1961 (Harper Torchbook).

———. *The Mycenaean Origin of Greek Mythology.* (Sather Classical Lectures, XIII.) Berkeley: Univ. of California Press, 1932 (Norton Library, 1963).

Norwood, Gilbert. *Pindar.* Berkeley: Univ. of California Press, 1909.

O'Sheridan, Mary Grant. *Gaelic Folk Tales.* Chicago: Hall and McCreary, 1909.

Ostwald, Martin. "Pindar, *Nomos,* and Heracles," *Harvard Studies in Classical Philology,* LXIX (1965), 109-138.

Bibliography

Parker, K. Langloh. *Australian Legendary Tales.* Sydney: Angus and Robertson, 1953 (reprinted 1954, 1955).

Puech, Aimé. *Pindare* (3rd ed.). 4 vols. Paris: Société D'Édition "Les Belles Lettres," 1961.

Radin, Paul. *Literary Aspects of North American Indian Mythology.* (Canada Geological Survey, Museum Bulletin No. 16, Anthropological Series No. 6.) Ottawa: Government Printing Bureau, 1915.

——. *The Trickster: A Study in American Indian Mythology* with commentaries by Karl Kerényi and C. G. Jung. London: Routledge and Kegan Paul, 1956.

Raglan, Lord [Fitz Roy Richard Somerset]. *The Hero: A Study in Tradition, Myth, and Drama.* New York: Oxford Univ. Press, 1937.

Rohde, Erwin. *Psyche.* English translation by W. B. Hillis. New York: Harcourt Brace, and Co., 1925.

Rooth, Anita Birgitta. "The Creation Myths of the North American Indians," *Anthropos,* 52 (1957), 497-508.

Rose, H. J. *Hygini Fabulae.* Leiden, 1934.

——. "The Grief of Persephone," *Harvard Theological Review,* XXXVI (1943).

——. *Handbook of Greek Literature* (3rd ed.). London: Methuen and Co. Ltd., 1948.

——. *A Handbook of Greek Mythology.* New York: E. P. Dutton and Co., 1960 (first published, 1928).

Sandys, Sir John E. *The Odes of Pindar.* London: William Heinemann, 1957.

Sebeok, Thomas A. (ed.). *Myth, a Symposium.* Bloomington: Indiana Univ. Press, 1955.

Seymour, Thomas D. *Selected Odes of Pindar.* Boston and New York: Ginn and Co., 1882.

Snell, Bruno. *Pindari Carmina cum Fragmentis: I. Pars prior, Epinicia* (4th ed.). II. *Pars altera, Fragmenta, Indices* (3rd ed.). Leipzig: Teubner, 1964.

Spencer, Katherine. *Mythology and Values: An Analysis of Navaho Chantway Myths.* Philadelphia: American Folklore Society, 1957.

Taylor, Archer. "The Biographical Pattern in Traditional Narrative," *Journal of the Folklore Institute,* I (1964).

Thompson, Stith. *Tales of the North American Indians.* Cambridge: Harvard Univ. Press, 1929.

141

Bibliography

————. *The Folktale.* New York: Dryden Press, 1951.

————. *Motif-Index of Folk-Literature.* Bloomington: Indiana Univ. Press, 1955.

————. *The Types of the Folktale: A Classification and Bibliography.* (FF Communications No. 184.) Helsinki: Suomalainen Tiedeakatemia, Academia Scientiarum Fennica, 1961. Translated and enlarged from Antti Aarne, *Verzeichnis der Märchentypen* (FF Communications No. 3).

Tolkien, J. R. R. *Tree and Leaf.* Boston: Houghton, Mifflin Co., 1965.

Trenkner, Sophie. *The Greek Novella in the Classical Period.* Cambridge: Cambridge Univ. Press, 1958.

Waterman, T. T. "The Explanatory Element in the Folk-Tales of the North American Indians," *Journal of American Folklore,* XXVII (1914), 1-54.

Webster, T. B. L. *From Mycenae to Homer* (2nd ed.). New York: W. W. Norton and Co., 1964.

Whitman, C. H. *Sophocles: A Study of Heroic Humanism.* Cambridge: Harvard Univ. Press, 1951.

Wilamowitz-Moellendorff, Ulrich von. *Pindaros.* Berlin, 1922.

Wimberly, Lowry Charles. *Folklore in the English and Scottish Ballads.* Chicago: Univ. of Chicago Press, 1928 (republished by Dover Publications, 1965).

Wright, W. C. *A Short History of Greek Literature from Homer to Julian.* New York: American Book Co., 1907.

Yourcenar, Marguerite. *Pindare.* Paris: Bernard Grasset, 1932.

Index of Motifs

An attempt to fit the motifs of Classical literature into the classifications of the Thompson *Motif-Index* presents difficulties at times. Though many are easily placed, others do not appear at all, or adjust awkwardly to the scheme. Tartarus, as distinct from Hades, for example, does not appear. Hades, for Pindar at least, cannot be accurately described as a "lower world of torment" or a "blessed place beneath the earth." One must assign the various activities of such complex divinities as Apollo, Zeus, and Athena to separate headings to represent them adequately; and many of the deeds of the gods, bestowal of immortality, transformations, and the like, seem to fall under the chapter head of Magic. Responses of the oracle, one of the most persistent motifs in Classical stories, must be divided between M. Ordaining the Future and D. Magic (Advice from the gods). Must Chiron, treated by Pindar almost as a god, be reduced to purely Centaur status under B. Unusual Animals, along with dragons and Harpies? Must Medea (as Circe, G 263.1) be classified as a witch and the various taskmasters, Aeëtes, for example, with a daughter who helps the hero, be classified as ogres (as Minos of Crete, G 530)? Of course small blame can be attached to the *Motif-Index*, which deals primarily with oral folktale traditions rather than with written literature, and these difficulties are often enlightening, pointing up differences of treatment between popular stories and those which have been modified by literary genius or poetic fancy. An examination of a single author confirms one's first impression that hundreds of new or similar motifs could be added from the large field of Classical mythology.

In this study the motifs under A, dealing with the Olympian gods, are suggestively rather than completely treated because of the great number of references. The motifs implied but not expressly given in Pindar's text are enclosed in parentheses. Asterisks mark tentative new entries.

A. Mythological Motifs

Gods

A 111 Parents of the gods.
> *Ol.* II. 12. 77; *Nem.* IX. 41; *Nem.* XI. 1; *Isth.* VIII. 45 Cronus and Rhea

A 111. 1 Mother of the gods.
> *Pyth.* III. 78; *Dith.* II Cybele

A 139 Nature and appearance of the gods, misc. (doubtful classification).
> *Nem.* I. 14; *Nem.* V. 34; *Isth.* VIII. 46 Nod of Zeus

A 141 God as craftsman. See A 451. 1 God of smith-work.

Ol. VII. 35; *Pyth.* I. 25; *Pyth.* III. 40; *Fr.* 283 Hephaestus

A 151. 1 Home of gods on high mountain.

Ol. II. 12; XIII. 92; *Nem.* X. 84; *Pae.* VI. 92 Olympus

A 154 Drink of the gods.

Pyth. IX. 63 Aristeas

A 154. 2 Theft of magic food.

Ol. I. 62 Tantalus

A 156. 5 Chariot of the gods.

Ol. IV. 1; *Ol.* VIII. 49; *Pyth.* IX. 6.

A 157. 1. 1 Thunderbolt as gods' weapon.

Nem. IX. 24.

A 157. 4 God's shield.

Isth. IV. 58 Aegis of Zeus

A 161. 1 Division of power among gods.

Ol. VII. 55 Assignment of Rhodes

A 161. 2 King of the gods.

Ol. IV. 1; *Nem.* V. 35; X. 16; *Isth.* VIII. 18 Zeus

A 161. 3 Queen of the gods.

Nem. I. 39; *Nem.* X. 18; *Pyth.* II. 27 Hera

A 162 Conflicts of the gods.

Pyth. VIII. 12 Typhon; *Pyth.* IV. 291 Freeing of Titans; *Fr.* 55 Python

A 162. 1 Fight of the gods and giants.

Nem. I. 67; *Pyth.* VIII. 12, 17; (*Isth.* VI. 32)

A 165. 1. 2 Eagle as god's bird.

Pyth. I. 6; *Pyth.* IV. 4.

A 165. 2 Messenger of the gods.

Ol. VI. 79; *Pyth.* IX. 59 Hermes

A 167. 1 Council of the gods.

Isth. VIII. 26.

A 169. 1 Judge and tribunal of the gods.

Isth. VIII. 24 Aeacus

A 178 God as prophet.

Ol. VIII. 41; *Pyth.* IV. 5 Apollo

A 179 Deeds of the gods, misc.

Pyth. III. 44 Apollo rescues unborn child; *Ol.* VII. 55-70 Apportionment of earth—Island of Rhodes; *Ol.* VII. 36 Birth of Athena; *Isth.* VIII. 27-46 Debate over marriage with Thetis; *Pae.* VI. 87-103 Debate over Troy

A 185 Deity cares for favorite individuals.

Ol. I. 87 Poseidon gives Pelops winged steeds; *Ol.* XIII. 65

Athena gives Bellerophon magic bridle; *Pyth.* IV. 213 Aphrodite brings wryneck to Jason

A 188 Gods and goddesses in love with men.

Pyth. IX. 5 ff. Apollo in love with Cyrene; see also T.

A 196. 1 Fate controls gods. See also Fates A 463. 1.

(*Ol.* III. 29 Fate binding Zeus and Heracles); *Pae.* VI. 94 Troy destined to fall

A 220 Sun-god.

Ol. VII. 14, 58, 71; *Pyth.* IV. 241; *Isth.* V. 1 Helius

A 240. 1 Moon-goddess.

Ol. III. 19 Mena (Selene)

A 270. 1 Goddess of Dawn.

Ol. 83; *Nem.* VI. 54 Eos

A 280 Weather-god.

Pyth. V. 9 Castor; *Fr.* 140c Tyndaridae

A 282 Wind-god.

Ol. III. 31; *Pyth.* IV. 181; *Fr. Parth.* II. 18 Boreas; *Pyth.* IV. 203 Notus

A 284 God of thunder.

Ol. IV. 1; *Pyth.* IV. 23 Zeus

A 310 God of the world of the dead.

Ol. IX. 33; *Pyth.* III. 11 Hades

A 310. 1 Goddess of world of the dead.

Ol. XIV. 20; *Pyth.* XII. 2; *Nem.* I. 14; *Isth.* VIII. 55 Persephone

A 311 Conductor of the dead.

Ol. IX. 33 Hades here instead of Hermes

A 401 Mother Earth.

Nem. VI. 1; *Ol.* VII. 38; *Pyth.* IX. 60, 102; *Fr.* 55

A 411. 4 Hearth-god (goddess).

Nem. XI. 1 Hestia

A 421 Sea-god.

Ol. I. 26, 72; *Ol.* VI. 103; *Pyth.* IV. 204 Poseidon; *Pyth.* IX. 14 Oceanus

A 421. 1 Sea-goddess.

Nem. III. 35; *Nem.* IV. 50 Thetis; *Ol.* II. 30; *Pyth.* XI. 2 Ino; *Ol.* VI. 105 Amphitrite

A 425 River-god.

Nem. I. 1 Alpheus

A 427. 1 Goddess of springs and wells.

Ol. XII. 19 Nymphs; *Pae.* II. 1 Naiad Thronia; *Dith.* II Naiades

A 433. 3 God of the vine.

Pae. IV. 25 Dionysus

A 441. 1 God of domestic beasts.

Ol. XIII. 69; *Ol.* V. 21; *Pyth.* IV. 45 Poseidon, Tamer of Horses

A. 451. 1 God of smith-work (see A 141 God as craftsman).

  (*Ol.* VII. 35 Hephaestus)

A 452. 1 Goddess of hunting.

  Nem. III. 50; *Ol.* III. 26; *Pyth.* IV. 90; *Dith.* II. 19 Artemis

A 453 Shepherd-god.

  Pyth. III. 78 Pan; *Pyth.* IX. 64 Aristeas

A 454 God of healing.

  Nem. III. 54; *Pyth.* III. 6, 46 Asclepius

*A 459. 2 God of athletics.

  Pyth. II. 10; *Isth.* I. 60 Hermes

A 461. 1 Goddess of wisdom.

  Ol. VII. 36, 51; *Pyth.* XII. 7; *Pae.* VI. 89 Athena (doubtful classification)

A 463. 1 The Fates (see A 482. 2 and N 111).

  Ol. I. 26; *Isth.* VI. 17 Clotho; *Ol.* VII. 64 Lachesis; *Ol.* II. 35; *Ol.* VI. 42; *Fr.* 30; *Nem.* VII. 1 Moira; see *Fr.* 41 Tyche as one of the Fates

A 464. 1 Goddess of justice.

  Ol. X. 13 Atrekia; *Ol.* XIII. 8 Themis

A 465. 0. 1 The Nine Muses.

  Pyth. I. 1; *Isth.* VIII. 58 Muses

A 465. 2 God of music.

  Pyth. I. 1 Apollo

A 468 The Three Graces.

  Ol. XIV. 1-18

A 471 God of prophecy.

  Pyth. IV. 5 Apollo at Delphi

A 474. 1. 1 Goddess of youth.

  Ol. VI. 58; *Nem.* VII. 4 Hebe

A 475. 0. 2 Marriage god.

  Thren. III. 7 (*Fr.* 139) Hymenaeus

A 475. 1 Goddess of love.

  Pyth. IV. 213-217; *Nem.* VIII. 1 Aphrodite

A 477 Goddess of childbirth.

  Nem. VII. 1-4 Eleithyia

A 482. 2 Goddess of good luck (Fortuna rather? See N 111).

  Ol. XII. 2; *Frr.* 39, 40, 41 Tyche

A 485 God of war.

  Pyth. I. 10-12 Ares

A 485. 1 Goddess of war.

  Dith. II. 17 Athena

A 486 The Furies.

Index of Motifs

Ol. II. 41 Erinnys

*A 496. 2 Goddesses of the seasons.

Ol. XIII. 17; *Pyth.* IX. 60 Horae

DEMIGODS AND CULTURE HEROES

A 515. 1. 1. 1 Twin culture heroes sired by two fathers.

Nem. X. 81-82; *Pyth.* IX. 85 Castor and Polydeuces; *Nem.* I. 36 Heracles and brother

A 541 Culture hero teaches arts and crafts.

Fr. 251 Aristeas; see A 453 Shepherd-god; A 1540 Heracles

COSMOGONY AND COSMOLOGY

A 651 Hierarchy of worlds (see 651. 2. 1 Two lower worlds).

(*Fr.* 207 Depths of Tartarus; *Pyth.* I. 15 Typhon in Tartarus; *Pae.* IV. 44 Euxantius); see A 310, A 311, A 671 Hades; A 151. 1 Olympus

A 657. 1 Bridge from earth to heaven.

Fr. 30

A 671 Hell. Lower world of torment.

Ol. II. 57, 67; *Pyth.* III. 11

A 671. 0. 3 Entrance to cave as gate to hell.

Pyth. IV. 44

A 672 Stygian river.

Pyth. XI. 21; *Nem.* IV. 85; *Fr.* 143 Acheron

A 675 Judges in the lower world.

Pyth. II. 73; *Ol.* II. 75 Rhadamanthus

A 690 Miscellaneous worlds.

Ol. II. 60-61; *Fr.* 129

A 692 Islands of the blest.

Nem. IV. 49; *Ol.* II. 70

A 772 Origin of Orion.

(*Nem.* II. 12); see F 531 Giants

A 773 Origin of the Pleiades.

Nem. II. 12; (*Frr.* 72, 73, 74); see R 321 Fugitives rise and become stars

A 841 Four world-columns.

(*Fr.* 33d Of Delos only)

A 842 Atlas.

Pyth. IV. 289

A 875. 1 Navel of the earth.

Pyth. IV. 4; *Pyth.* VI. 3; *Pyth.* VIII. 59; *Pyth.* XI. 10; *Nem.* VII. 33; *Fr.* 54; see A 165. 1. 2 Eagle as god's bird

TOPOGRAPHICAL FEATURES OF THE EARTH.

A 930 Origin of Streams.

(*Pyth.* IV. 138 Poseidon of the Rock—splitting of Tempe)

147

A 941. 0. 1 Origin of a particular spring.

Isth. VI. 74 Spring of Dirce

A 955 Origin of islands.

Ol. VII. 56 ff. Rhodes

A 955. 10 Islands from transformed object or person.

Pae. V. 40-41 Delos

A 966 Origin of volcanoes.

Pyth. I. 16 ff.; *Ol.* IV. 8; *Fr.* 92 Aetna over Typhon

A 984 Pillars of Heracles

Ol. III. 44; *Nem.* III. 21; *Isth.* IV. 12

WORLD CALAMITIES

A 1010 Deluge.

Ol. IX. 50 ff.

A 1022 Escape from deluge on mountain.

Ol. IX. 43 Deucalion and Pyrrha

CREATION AND ORDERING OF HUMAN LIFE

A 1224. 7 Creation of men by creator from ants.

(*Nem.* III. 13; *Pae.* VI. 107 Myrmidons)

A 1234 Mankind emerges from ground. See T 545.

Fr. 253 Erechthonius (Erechtheus? *Pyth.* VII. 10)

A 1245. 1 New race from stones thrown after deluge.

Ol. IX. 45 By Deucalion and Pyrrha

A 1265 Men created from sown dragon's teeth.

Pyth. IX. 82; *Isth.* I. 30; *Isth.* VII. 10; *Fr.* 29 Sparti

A 1445 Acquisition of building crafts.

Ol. XIII. 21 Pediments

A 1460 Acquisition of arts.

Fr. 139. 3 Invention of dithyramb

A 1461 Acquisition of music.

Pyth. XII. 7, 20 Invention of flute harmony; see F 526. 3 Gorgon;
Fr. 125 Lydian harmony; (*Nem.* IV. 45)

A 1545 Origin of sacrifices.

Ol. VII. 48 Fireless sacrifices at Rhodes

A 1549. 3 Origin of religious games.

Ol. II. 3; *Ol.* III. 19, 20; *Ol.* VI. 69; *Ol.* X. 25; *Nem.* X. 33; *Nem.*
XI. 27 Olympic Games by Heracles; *Nem.* X. 28 Games at
Nemea by Adrastus; *Nem.* IX. 9; *Isth.* IV. 26 Games at Sicyon by
Adrastus; *Fr.* 5. 3 at Isthmus by Sisyphus

A 1577 Origin of personal names.

Ol. VI. 57 Iamus from pansies; *Isth.* VI. 53 Ajax from eagle;
(*Fr.* 291 Alcides to Heracles); *Fr.* 75. 10; 85c Dionysus

148

Index of Motifs

B 535. 0. 14 Serpent as nurse for child.

   Ol. VI. 46, 47 Serpents feed Iamus

B 559 Animals carry men, misc.

   Pyth. IV. 161 Phrixus on Ram with golden fleece

MARRIAGE OF PERSON TO ANIMAL

B 611. 3 Horse paramour.

   Pyth. II. 45 Centaurus with Magnesian mares

C. TABU

TABU CONNECTED WITH SUPERNATURAL BEINGS

C 51. 5 Tabu: imitating god.

   Pyth. III. 56 Asclepius restores man to life (*Pyth.* IV. 143 Salmoneus?)

C 52 Tabu: being in presence of god.

   Ol. II. 26 Semele

SEX TABU

C 191 Tabu: mortal lusting after goddess.

   Pyth. II. 36 Ixion for Hera; *Pyth.* IV. 92 Tityus for Artemis

MISCELLANEOUS TABUS

*C 770. 2 Tabu: attempt to fly to heaven.

   (*Ol.* XIII. 91); *Isth.* VII. 46 Bellerophon; see L 421 Attempt to fly to heaven punished

C 771. 2 Tabu: piling up mountains to reach heaven.

   Fr. 162 Otus and Ephialtes

D. MAGIC

TRANSFORMATION

D 101 Transformation: god to animal.

   Fr. 91 Gods change to escape Typhon

D 114. 1. 1, 2 Transformation: woman to doe.

   Ol. III. 29 Taygete

D 127. 5 Transformation: man to dolphin.

   (*Fr.* 236)

D 133. 1 Transformation to cow.

   (*Fr.* 51f Io)

D 133. 2 Transformation: man to bull.

   (*Fr.* 249a Achelous)

D 235. 1 Transformation: man (god) to shower of gold.

   Pyth. XII. 17 Zeus at conception of Perseus

D 284 Transformation: woman to island.

   Pae. V. 42 Asterie to Delos

D 550 Transformation by drinking.

(*Fr.* 263 Glaucus; cf. Paus. IX. 22. 7)

D 581 Petrification by glance.

Pyth. X. 48; (*Dith.* IV. 41) Gorgon Medusa

D 642. 3 Transformation to escape lover.

Nem. IV. 62; *Nem.* III. 35 Thetis; *Ol.* III. 29 Taygete; (*Pyth.* III. 69 Arethusa; cf. *Nem.* I. 1 Alpheus in pursuit of Arethusa)

D 658 Transformation to seduce woman.

Nem. X. 13-17; (*Isth.* VII. 5-6) Zeus to Amphitryon

D 671 Transformation flight.

Fr. 91 Gods to animals; see D. 101

*D 690 Transformation, misc.

Pyth. IV. 29 Triton? as Eurypylus

Magic Objects

D 903 Magic snow.

Ol. VII. 34, 50 Rhodes; *Isth.* VII. 5-6 birth of Heracles; *Fr.* 119? Rhodes?

D 1065. 5 Magic sandals.

(*Fr.* 269 Bowra; cf. Apollod. II. 4. 2 Perseus)

D 1081 Magic sword (knife).

Nem. IV. 59 Peleus

D 1193 Magic bag.

(*Fr.* 269 Bowra; cf. Apollod. II. 4. 2 Perseus)

D 1209. 1 Magic bridle.

Ol. XIII. 65 For Pegasus

D 1254. 1 Magic wand.

Ol. IX. 33 Wand of Hades; *Pyth.* IV. 178, *Dith.* IV. 37 Wand of Hermes

D 1344. 2. 1 Magic drug gives immunity from fire.

Pyth. IV. 221 Jason and bulls

D 1355 Love-producing magic object.

Pyth. IV. 214 Iynx to win Medea

D 1400. 1. 4. 5 Hercules' bow and arrows essential to capture Troy.

(*Pyth.* I. 53 Heracles' bow and arrows)

D 1413. 6 Chair to which person sticks.

Fr. 283 Hephaestus for Hera

D 1470. 2. 3 Horn of plenty.

(*Dith.* II; *Fr.* 249a)

D 1553 Symplegades.

Pyth. IV. 208 Clashing Islands

D 1620 Magic automata.

Ol. VII. 52 Made by Telchines?; *Fr.* 282 Statue in Egypt

151

MAGIC POWERS AND MANIFESTATIONS

D 1711 Magician.

Pyth. IV. 221 Medea; *Ol.* VII. 52 Telchines?

D 1812. 3. 3 Future revealed in dream.

Pae. VIIIa. 17 Hecuba

D 1812. 5. 0. 3 Behavior of fire as omen.

Ol. VIII. 3

D 1812. 5. 1 Bad omens.

Nem. IX. 19 Amphiaraus

D 1812. 5. 2 Favorable omens.

Ol. X. 80; *Pyth.* IV. 23, 197 Thunder of Zeus; *Pae.* II. 78 Hecate; *Pyth.* IV. 191 Birds and lots; *Isth.* VI. 50 Eagle; see D 1812. 5. 0. 2 Omens from flight of birds

D 1814. 3 Advice from god (or gods).

Ol. XIII. 66 Athena to Bellerophon; *Ol.* VII. 32 Tlepolemus told to go to Rhodes; *Pyth.* IV. 164 Pelias told to bring Phrixus' spirit home

D 1840 Magic invulnerability.

Fr. 167, *Thren.* VI. Caeneus; *Isth.* III. 18 Sons of gods; *Isth.* VI. 48? Ajax

D 1841. 3 Burning magically evaded.

Pyth. III. 44 Apollo

D 1850. 2 Woman changes into an immortal.

Ol. II. 30; *Pyth.* XI. 2 Ino

D 1851 Immortality bestowed.

Ol. III. 36; *Nem.* I. 72; *Isth.* IV. 55 Heracles; *Ol.* II. 78; *Nem.* IV. 65 Peleus; *Ol.* II. 78 Cadmus; *Ol.* II. 79 Achilles; *Ol.* II. 26; *Pyth.* XI. 1 Semele

D 1851. 5 Immortality bestowed by deity.

Ol. I. 25, 42 Pelops; *Ol.* I. 44 Ganymede; *Nem.* X. 7 Diomede

*D 1852 Immortality withdrawn by deity.

Ol. I. 65 ff. Pelops (possibly C 937. 1 Tabu: Immortality lost by breach of tabu)

D 1853. 1 Immortality exchanged for death on alternate days.

Pyth. XI. 63; *Nem.* X. 55, 87-88 Castor and Polydeuces

E. THE DEAD

RESUSCITATION

E 15. 1 Resuscitation by boiling.

Ol. I. 26, 50 Pelops; see also E 33 Resuscitation with missing member, and E 121. 1. 1 Resuscitation by concerted effort of gods

E 50 Resuscitation by magic.

Pyth. III. 57 Asclepius; see Tabu

E 121. 1 Resuscitation by a god.

Nem. X. 90 Castor by Zeus (or Polydeuces?); (*Pyth.* IX. 81 Iolaus)

GHOSTS AND OTHER REVENANTS

E 230 Return from dead to inflict punishment.

(*Pyth.* IX. 81 Iolaus)

E 481 Land of the dead.

Ol. XIV. 21; *Isth.* VIII. 55; *Fr.* 133 Home of Persephone; *Ol.* VIII. 72; IX. 33; X. 92; *Pyth.* III. 11; IV. 44; V. 96; *Nem.* VII. 31; *Isth.* I. 68 Hades

*E 499.5 Dead in lower world rejoice in news of living.

Pyth. V. 101; *Nem.* IV. 85; *Ol.* XIV. 22; *Ol.* VIII. 77

E 545. 18 Ghost asks to be taken to former home.

Pyth. IV. 159 Phrixus

REINCARNATION

E 600 Reincarnation.

Ol. II. 69; *Fr.* 133

THE SOUL

E 720. 1 Souls of human beings seen in dream.

Fr. 131b

F. MARVELS

OTHER WORLD JOURNEYS

F 2 Translation to other world without dying.

Fr. 167, *Thren.* VI Caeneus; *Ol.* VI. 14; *Nem.* IX. 25 Amphiaraus; *Ol.* II. 78-79 Peleus, Cadmus, Achilles

F 52 Ladder to uper world.

Fr. 30 Themis to heaven

F 81 Descent to lower world of dead.

Dith. II, *Fr.* 70b Heracles

F 110 Journey to terrestrial other worlds. See F 111 Journey to earthly paradise, and D 1338. 7 Land of youth.

Pyth. X. 30-44; *Ol.* III. 16; *Isth.* VI. 23; *Fr.* 272b; *Fr.* 270 Abaris and Hyperboreans

MARVELOUS CREATURES

F 420. 4. 10 Water-spirits are prophetic.

Pyth. III. 92 Nereus

F 423. 1 Nereid (Thetis).

Pyth. XI. 2; *Nem.* IV. 65; *Isth.* VI. 6

F 441. 2. 2 Dryad.

Fr. 165 Rhoecus and Dryad

153

F 500 Remarkable persons.
 Isth. I. 13; *Fr.* 169. 6 Geryon; see G. Ogres

F 512. 1. 1 Person with one eye in center of forehead.
 Fr. 266

F 512. 1. 2 Three women have but one eye among them, pass it around.
 (*Pyth.* XII. 13 Graeae)

*F 522. 2 Person with wings on back.
 Pyth. IV. 183 Sons of Boreas

F 526. 1 Typhon.
 Ol. IV. 7; *Pyth.* I. 16; *Pyth.* VIII. 16; *Fr.* 91; *Fr.* 93 Typhon

F 526. 3 Gorgon.
 Ol. XIII. 63; *Pyth.* X. 46; *Pyth.* XII. 7, 16; *Nem.* X. 4 Gorgon Medusa

F 531 Giants.
 Pyth. VIII. 12, 17 Porphyrion; *Pyth.* IV. 90 Tityus; *Pyth.* IV. 289 Atlas; *Nem.* I. 65; *Isth.* IV. 52 Antaeus (both the same?); *Isth.* IV. 49; *Nem.* II. 12; *Frr.* 72, 73, 74 Orion; *Nem.* IV. 27; *Isth.* VI. 33 Alcyoneus; *Nem.* I. 67; *Nem.* VII. 90 Giants; *Ol.* X. 16 Cycnus and Heracles; *Isth.* V. 39 Cycnus and Achilles; *Pyth.* IV. 89; *Fr.* 162 Otus and Ephialtes; *Ol.* X. 27-28 **Moliones**

F 565. 1 Amazons.
 Ol. VIII. 47; *Ol.* XIII. 87-89; *Nem.* III. 38; *Fr.* 172 (girdle of Queen) Amazons

F 565. 4 Woman hunters.
 Pyth. IX. 21, 26 Cyrene

F 601 Extraordinary companions.
 Pyth. IV. 170-187 Argonauts

F 611. 3. 2 Hero's precocious strength.
 Nem. III. 44-47 Achilles; *Nem.* I. 43-45 Heracles; see F 628. 1. 3. 2

F 614. 10 Hero fights whole army alone.
 Nem. III. 34 Peleus conquers Iolcus

F 628. 1. 3. 2 Child tears to pieces a live snake with his bare hands.
 Nem. I. 43-45 Heracles

F 642. 3. 1 Person of remarkable sight (can see through trees).
 Nem. X. 62 Lynceus

*F 679. 9. 1 Skillful musician as friend of hero.
 Pyth. IV. 177 Orpheus

EXTRAORDINARY PLACES AND THINGS

F 715. 3. 1 Undersea river.
 (*Nem.* I. 1 Alpheus)

F 736 Island with extraordinary support.
 Fr. 33d Delos

F 771. 1. 9 House of skulls.

Isth. IV. 54 Temple of Antaeus

F 824 Extraordinary armor.

Nem. VIII. 27 Golden armor

F 834 Extraordinary spear.

Nem. III. 33 Spear of Peleus

EXTRAORDINARY OCCURRENCES

F 900 Extraordinary occurrences.

Pyth. IV. 26 Carrying *Argo* twelve days; *Pyth*. V. 58 Lions flee Battus

G. OGRES

KINDS OF OGRES

G 200 Witch.

Pyth. IV. 221 Medea gives drugs to Jason; see M 301 Prophets

G 311 Old man of the sea.

Pyth. IX. 94 Nereus, old man of the sea; see A 421

OGRE DEFEATED

G 530. 2 Help from ogre's daughter.

Pyth. IV. 221 Medea gives drugs to Jason

H. TESTS

IDENTITY TESTS: RECOGNITION

H 51. 1 Recognition by birthmark.

Ol. I. 27 Pelops—shoulder

*H 119. 3 Recognition by one sandal.

Pyth. IV. 75, 96 Jason by Pelias; see M 341. 2. 9

MARRIAGE TESTS

H 331 Suitor contest: bride offered as prize.

Pyth. IX. 106 Race for daughter of Antaeus; *Pyth*. IX. 112 Danaus plans contest for daughters

H 331. 5. 2 Suitor contest: race with bride's father.

Ol. I. 75 ff.; *Ol*. IX. 9 Pelops with Oenomaus

H 331. 6. 1 Suitor contest: wrestling with bride.

Nem. III. 35; *Nem*. IV. 62-65 Peleus and Thetis

*H 331. 6. 2 Wrestling with bull-shaped river-god.

(*Fr*. 249a Achelous)

TESTS OF PROWESS: TASKS

H 901. 1 Heads on stakes for failure.

(*Ol*. I. 79 Death of suitors of Hippodameia); also *Fr*. 135

H 1102 Task: cleaning Augean stable.

Ol. X. 28

H 1133. 5 Task: building city.

Ol. VIII. 32 Aeacus to help build Troy

H 1150 Task: stealing, capturing, or slaying.

Ol. XIII. 85 Pegasus; *Nem.* I. 63; *Nem.* III. 23 Heracles and monsters; *Isth.* IV. 53 Heracles and Antaeus; *Ol.* XIII. 87-89; *Nem.* III. 38; *Fr.* 172 Amazons

H 1151. 5 Task: stealing belt from queen.

Fr. 172 Heracles from queen of Amazons; see H 1150

H 1151. 8 Task: stealing cattle.

Isth. I. 13; *Fr.* 169 Cattle of Geryon; (*Isth.* VI. 32 Alcyoneus "herdsman" and cattle of the sun; Farnell, II, 360)

H 1161 Task: killing ferocious beast.

(*Nem.* VI. 44); *Isth.* VI. 37, 48; *Isth.* III. 12; (*Ol.* XIII. 44) Nemean Lion

H 1174. 2 Task: overcoming dragon.

Pyth. IV. 249 Jason and Dragon; *Ol.* XIII. 90 Chimera by Bellerophon; see B 11. 11

TESTS OF PROWESS: QUESTS

H 1210 Quest assigned.

Pyth. IV. 165 Golden fleece; *Ol.* III. 29 Hind with golden antlers; see B 101. 4

H 1215 Quest assigned because of hero's boast.

See H 1332. 3 Gorgon's head

H 1332. 1 Quest for golden fleece.

Pyth. IV. 165

H 1332. 3 Quest for head of Gorgon.

Pyth. X. 46; *Pyth.* XII. 7, 16; *Nem.* X. 4; *Dith.* IV Perseus; see F 526. 3 Gorgon

OTHER TESTS

H 1561. 6 Tests of valor: fight with giant.

Nem. IV. 27; *Isth.* VI. 33; *Nem.* I. 67 Heracles and Alcyoneus; *Ol.* X. 16 Cycnus, son of Ares, and Heracles; *Pyth.* VIII. 12, 17 Porphyrion and Heracles; *Isth.* IV. 54 Antaeus; *Pyth.* IX. 106 Antaeus; *Nem.* VII. 90 Giants

H 1568 Test of the champion.

Nem. VII. 25; *Nem.* VIII. 26 Contest for arms of Achilles

H 1598 Contest between man and other being.

Ol. IX. 30-34 Heracles against three gods

K. DECEPTIONS

DECEPTIVE BARGAINS

K 231. 1 Refusal to perform part in mutual agreement.

Ol. X. 28 Augeas; *Isth.* VI. 29; *Fr.* 140a. 66 Laomedon

156

Index of Motifs

L. REVERSAL OF FORTUNE

Isth. IV. 53 Heracles, small of stature, against Antaeus; *Pyth.* I. 55 Philoctetes

PRIDE BROUGHT LOW

L 400　Pride brought low.

　　Ol. XIII. 10 Hybris

L 410　Proud ruler (deity) humbled.

　　Ol. I. 88 Oenomaus; *Pyth.* XII. 14 Polydectes

L 421　Attempt to fly to heaven punished.

　　Isth. VII. 44-47 Bellerophon; see C 770. 2

M. ORDAINING THE FUTURE

JUDGMENTS AND DECREES

M 10　Irrevocable Judgments (see Fate).

　　Ol. IX. 42, 52 Ordinance of Zeus draws off flood; *Isth.* VII. 15; *Pyth.* IV. 7, 60; *Pyth.* V. 68 Pytho (Delphi) as seat of oracles; *Pyth.* XI. 6 Ismenian shrine; *Nem.* I. 13; *Nem.* V. 34 Promise of Zeus; *Pae.* VI. 94, 114 Destruction of Troy ordained; *Fr.* 58 Oracle revealed by dove at Dodona

VOWS AND OATHS

M 119. 1. 1　Oath by River Styx.

　　Ol. VII. 65 Great oath of gods; *Ol.* III. 29 Oath implied

PROPHECIES

M 301　Prophets.

　　Ol. VI. 66 Iamus; *Pyth.* VIII. 60 Alcmaeon; *Pyth.* IX. 51 ff. Chiron; *Isth.* VII. 8; *Nem.* I. 60 ff. Tiresias; *Pae.* IV. 28-29 Melampus; *Pae.* VII. 13; *Pae.* IX. 41 Tenerus; *Pyth.* IV. 11 Medea; *Ol.* XIII. 75 Polyidus; *Pyth.* VIII. 39 Amphiaraus; *Pyth.* IV. 191 Mopsus

M 301. 0. 1　Prophet destined never to be believed.

　　Pyth. XI. 33 Cassandra; *(Pae.* VIII. 10 Cassandra)

M 302. 7　Prophecy through dreams.

　　Pae. VIII. 17 Hecuba; *Pyth.* IV. 163 Pelias

M 311. 0. 1　Heroic career prophesied for new-born child.

　　Nem. I. 61 ff. Tiresias for Heracles; *Isth.* VI. 53 ff. Heracles for Ajax

M 312　Prophecy of future greatness for youth.

　　Ol. VI. 37, 48, 49-51 Iamus

M 312. 2. 1　Prophecy: son to be greater than father.

　　Isth. VIII. 33 Of Achilles

M 314. 4　Prophecy of future empire for fugitives.

　　Pyth. IV. 13-56 Medea for Argonauts

M 340　Unfavorable prophecies.

Nem. VII. 44; *Pae.* VI. 112 Neoptolemus

M 341. 2. 9 Prophecy: death from man wearing one sandal.

Pyth. IV. 75 Jason

M 343 Parricide prophecy.

Ol. II. 38; *Fr.* 68 Laius

M 356. 1 Prophecies concerning outcome of war.

Ol. VIII. 37 ff. Snakes at wall of Troy and Apollo's prophecy;
Pyth. I. 55 Heracles' arrows at Troy; see Z 312 and Z 358

M 356. 1. 1 Prophecy: loss of battle.

Fr. 140a. 66 Laomedon

M 356. 1. 2 Prophecies concerning fate of heroes in battle.

Pyth. VIII. 40 ff. Amphiaraus in oracle at his tomb

N. Chance and Fate

The Ways of Luck and Fate

N 111 Fortuna (see A 482. 2 and A 463. 1 Fate).

Ol. XII. 2-12; *Frr.* 39, 40, 41 Tyche

N 130 Changing of luck or fate.

Ol. II. 23 Daughters of Cadmus; *Ol.* II. 37 ff. Oedipus and sons;
Pyth. III. 86-103 Cadmus and Peleus; *Pyth.* III. 82-83 Gods as
dispensers of good and evil

N 170 The capriciousness of luck or fate.

Fr. 40 Tyche

Unlucky Accidents

N 340. 1 Suicide.

Nem. VII. 26; *Nem.* VIII. 23, 27; *Isth.* IV. 36 Ajax

Accidental Encounters

N 733. 1 Brothers unwittingly fight each other.

Ol. II. 42 Eteocles and Polynices; *Fr.* 163 Otus and Ephialtes

P. Society

Royalty and Nobility

P 12. 2. 1 Tyrannical king.

Pyth. IV. 110 Pelias takes Jason's lands

P 17. 10 Three sons each get kingship.

Ol. VII. 75 ff. Division of Rhodes

The Family

P. 251. 5. 3 Hostile brothers.

Ol. II. 42 Sons of Oedipus

Government

P 557. 6 Warrior dies facing foe.

Nem. IX. 26 Amphiaraus

Index of Motifs

Q. REWARDS AND PUNISHMENTS

NATURE OF REWARDS

Q 150. 1 Rescue from deluge as reward.

Ol. IX. 42 Deucalion and Pyrrha

Q 172. 9 Deification as reward.

Pyth. XI. 1-2; *Ol.* II. 25-29 Semele and Ino; *Nem.* X. 7 Diomede; *Pyth.* XI. 63; *Nem.* X. 55, 86-90 Castor and Polydeuces (see D 1853.1); *Nem.* I. 71; *Nem.* X. 18; *Isth.* IV. 59 Heracles (see D 1851. 5)

DEEDS PUNISHED

Q 200 Deeds punished.

Pyth. XI. 37 Aegisthus and Clytemnestra slain; *Pyth.* IX. 81 Eurystheus beheaded; *Pyth.* IV. 250 Pelias slain by Medea; *Pyth.* XII. 14 Polydectes slain by Perseus; *Ol.* I. 88 Oenomaus slain by Pelops; *Pae.* VI. 112 ff. Neoptolemus not to return home

Q 221 Personal offences against gods punished.

Pyth. IV. 92 Love of Tityus for Artemis; *Pyth.* II. 27, 34 Ixion for Hera; see Q 501. 5

Q 255 Punishment of woman who prefers mortal lover.

Pyth. III. 8 ff. Coronis

Q 331 Pride punished.

Isth. VII. 46; *Ol.* XIII. 91 Bellerophon

KINDS OF PUNISHMENT

Q 411 Death as punishment.

Ol. I. 79 Suitors of Hippodamia (heads on stakes?); *Fr.* 266 Cyclopes

Q 431 Punishment: banishment.

Ol. VII. 32 Tlepolemus; *Nem.* V. 14-16 Peleus and Telamon

Q 434 Punishment: fettering.

Pyth. I. 16 Typhon under Etna and in Tartarus

Q 501. 2 Punishment of Tantalus.

Ol. I. 57; *Isth.* VIII. 10 Tantalus

Q 501. 5 Punishment of Ixion.

Pyth. II. 22, 40-41 Ixion

Q 552. 1 Death by thunderbolt as punishment.

Pyth. VIII. 16, 17 Typhon and Giants; *Nem.* X. 71 Idas and Lynceus; *Ol.* II. 26 Semele; *Pyth.* III. 57 Asclepius; *Nem.* IX. 25; *Nem.* X. 8; *Ol.* VI. 14 Amphiaraus

Q 552. 10 Plague as punishment.

Pyth. III. 36 Countrymen of Coronis (see Q 255)

Q 555 Madness as punishment.

(*Ol.* II. 30 Ino)

160

Index of Motifs

R. Captives and Fugitives

CAPTIVITY

R 13. 3. 2 Eagle carries off youth.

(*Ol.* I. 44 Ganymede)

R 14 Deity abducts person.

Pyth. IX. 6 Cyrene by Apollo; *Isth.* VIII. 21; *Pae.* VI. 137 Aegina by Zeus; *Ol.* IX. 58 Daughter of Opus by Zeus; *Ol.* I. 41-42 Pelops by Poseidon

RESCUES

R 154. 2 Sons rescues father.

Pyth. VI. 39 Nestor by son

R 169 Other rescuers.

Isth. VIII. 52 Achilles for Helen; *Nem.* VII. 28 Ajax for Helen, etc.

R 169. 13 Child rescued by nurse.

Pyth. XI. 17 Orestes

R 170 Miscellaneous rescues.

Pyth. IV. 161 Phrixus by ram

ESCAPES AND PURSUITS

R 210 Escapes

Nem. IX. 13 Adrastus

R 260 Pursuits.

Nem. I. 1 Alpheus for Arethusa

REFUGES AND RECAPTURE

R 311 Tree refuge.

Nem. X. 62 For Dioscuri

R 321 Escape to the stars.

(*Nem.* II. 12 Pleiades)

S. Unnatural Cruelty

CRUEL RELATIVES

S 11. 3 Father kills child.

Pyth. XI. 23 Iphigenia by Agamemnon; *Ol.* I. 49 Pelops by Tantalus; (*Isth.* IV. 63 Sons by Heracles?)

S 31 Cruel stepmother.

Nem. I. 40 Hera sends snakes against Heracles; *Pyth.* IV. 162 Phrixus saved from stepmother

S 60 Cruel spouse.

Pyth. XI. 19 Clytemnestra murders Agamemnon and Cassandra; *Pyth.* IV. 252 Lemnian women kill husbands; (*Nem.* X. 6 Danaids kill husbands?—see T 173. 2)

S 73. 1. 0. 1 Murder of stepbrother.

161

(*Nem.* V. 14 Phocus by Peleus and Telamon)

REVOLTING MURDERS OR MUTILATIONS

S 110 Murders.

Isth. IV. 54 Antaeus slaying strangers, using skulls; *Fr.* 140a. 56 Laomedon, stranger-murdering

S 112 Burning to death.

Pyth. I. 96 Phalaris' brazen bull; (*Pyth.* II. 32 Ixion's crime against Deioneus)

S 145 Abandonment on an island.

Pyth. I. 53 Philoctetes on Lemnos

ABANDONED OR MURDERED CHILDREN

S 301 Children abandoned (exposed).

Ol. VI. 45 Iamus by Evadne

CRUEL PERSECUTIONS

S 400 Cruel persecutions.

Pyth. IV. 114 Jason as baby sent away from Pelias; *Pyth.* XI. 16 Orestes from mother; *Pyth.* XII. 14-15 Persecution of Perseus and Danae (see H 1332. 3 Quest for head of Gorgon)

T. SEX

LOVE

T 92 Rivals in love.

Isth. VIII. 27 Gods rivals for Thetis

MARRIAGE

T 111. 1 Marriage of a mortal and a god.

Nem. X. 11, 17 Zeus, Alcmene, Danae; *Pyth.* IV. 172 Zeus, Alcmene, Leda; *Isth.* VII. 7; *Pyth.* IX. 84 Zeus, Alcmene; *Ol.* II. 27; *Pyth.* III. 99 Zeus, Semele; *Isth.* VIII. 21; *Nem.* VII. 84; *Nem.* VIII. 6; *Pae.* VI. 137 Zeus, Aegina; *Isth.* VIII. 19 (Zeus, Thebe); *Ol.* III. 29 (Zeus, Taygete); *Pyth.* III. 14 Apollo, Coronis; *Pyth.* IX. 28 ff. Apollo, Cyrene; (*Pae.* VIIa. 4); *Pae.* IX. 35, 43 Apollo, Melia; *Fr.* 51c Apollo, Zeuxippe; *Nem.* X. 18; *Nem.* I. 71; *Isth.* IV. 60 Heracles, Hebe; *Isth.* VI. 25; *Pyth.* III. 92; *Nem.* III. 35, 56; *Nem.* IV. 65; *Nem.* V. 25, 36 Peleus, Thetis; *Pyth.* III. 91 Cadmus, Harmonia

T 173. 2 Hostile brides kill husbands in the bridal bed.

(*Nem.* X. 6 Daughters of Danaus kill husbands)

MARRIED LIFE

T 210 Faithfulness in marriage.

Nem. X. 6 Hypermnestra

T 230 Faithlessness in marriage.

Pyth. III. 25 ff. Coronis; *Pyth.* XI. 24 Clytemnestra; (*Nem.* IX. 16 Eriphyle)

Index of Motifs

ILLICIT SEXUAL RELATIONS

T 463 Homosexual love.

Ol. I. 25, 41 Poseidon and Pelops; *Ol.* I. 44 Zeus and Ganymede

CONCEPTION AND BIRTH

T 510 Miraculous conception (see Z 216).

Pyth. XII. 16 Perseus by golden shower; *Isth.* VII. 7 Heracles (imitation of Perseus)

T 540 Miraculous birth.

Pyth. II. 45 Centaurus from cloud; *Pyth.* II. 46 Centaurs from Centaurus and mares

T 541 Birth from unusual part of person's body.

Ol. VII. 36 Athena from head of Zeus; *Fr.* 34 Athena

T 545 Birth from ground.

(*Pyth.* VII. 10 Erechtheus)

T 549 Miraculous birth, miscellaneous.

Isth. I. 30 Sparti, from dragon's teeth (see A 1265), from stones (see A 1245. 1)

CARE OF CHILDREN

T 685. 1 Twin adventurers (see Z 210 Brothers as heroes).

Ol. X. 34 Moliones; *Fr.* 161 Cercopes; see Z 210 for Castor and Polydeuces, and Idas and Lynceus, all four in *Nem.* X. 60-90

Z. MISCELLANEOUS GROUPS OF MOTIFS

FORMULAS

Z 71. 1 Formulistic number: three.

Nem. III. 33-35 Three tasks of Peleus

*Z 71. 1. 19 Three Graces.

Ol. XIV. 1-18 (The three are named, though the number three does not appear)

Z 71. 5 Formulistic number: seven.

Ol. VI. 15; *Nem.* IX. 24 Seven pyres for Seven against Thebes; *Pyth.* III. 91; VIII. 40; XI. 11; *Nem.* IV. 19; *Nem.* IX. 18; *Isth.* I. 67; VIII. 15 Seven-gated Thebes

*Z 71. 16. 17 Formulistic number: fifty.

Isth. VI. 6 Nereids; *Nem.* X. 1 Daughters of Danaus

*Z 71. 16. 18 Formulistic number: one hundred.

Ol. IV. 7; *Pyth.* VIII. 16 Typhon; *Fr.* 249b Cerberus; *Pae.* VIIIa. 21 Hecatoncheires

SYMBOLISM

Z 110 Personifications.

Ol. II. 17; X. 55 Time; *Ol.* XIII. 10 Hybris, Corus (Surfeit);

Pyth. VIII. 1 Hesychia (Calm); and many more (see Farnell, II, 467)

*Z 187 Symbol of rule over land.

Pyth. IV. 34 Clod as symbol

*Z 188 Symbol of destruction of fortress.

Ol. VIII. 36 Serpents climbing wall of Troy

HEROES

Z 210 Brothers as heroes (see T 685. 1 Twin adventurers).

Nem. X. 50-90 *passim* Castor and Polydeuces; Idas and Lynceus

Z 211 Dreadnaughts.

Fr. 29. 4 Heracles "all-daring"; Ol. VI. 67 "bold in counsel"

Z 216 Supernatural origin of hero.

Pyth. XII. 16 Perseus from shower of gold (see T 510)

Z 231 Boyish exploits of hero.

Nem. III. 43 Achilles; Nem. I. 43-45 Heracles (See F 611 and 628)

Z 292 Death of hero.

Nem. VIII. 30; Isth. VIII. 36 Achilles; Nem. VII. 26; Nem. VIII. 23, 27; Isth. IV. 36 Ajax

UNIQUE EXCEPTIONS

Z 310 Unique vulnerability.

Fr. 167 (*Thren.* VI) Caeneus; (*Isth.* VI. 47? Ajax)

Z 312 Unique deadly weapon.

Fr. 167 (*Thren.* VI) Fir trees against Caeneus; (*Pyth.* I. 50 Heracles' bow held by Philoctetes, against Troy)

*Z 358 Unique victim.

Pyth. VIII. 52 Adrastus' son

*Z 359 Unique example.

Pyth. IV. 210-211 Passage of *Argo* stops movement of Clashing Islands; *Pae.* VI. 114 Slayer of Priam never to go home; Troy could not be taken without Neoptolemus.

Index of Mythological Characters

Abaris, 23, 114n55

Acastus, 95, 96

Achelous, 119n116

Achilles: his youth with Chiron, 3, 11, 28, 97, 102, 110n6, 135 n126; description and characterization of, 10, 34, 38, 52, 121n143; in modern surveys, 10, 119n121; in the *Iliad*, 19, 21, 52, 83; speaking horse of, 26, 85, 115n65; spear of, 33, 117n78; friend of Patroclus, 35; death and translation to Elysium of, 48, 75, 120n130, 130n63; folktale elements in stories about, 88, 132n93, 134n105, 135n118

Admetus, 44

Adrastus: in war against Thebes, 24, 26, 87, 115n65; founds Nemean Games, 122n1

Aeacus, 45, 88

Aeëtes, 11, 66

Aegialeus, 87

Aegina: her union with Zeus praised, 50, 91, 118n105, 121n134

Aegisthus, 55

Aepytus, 86

Agamedes, 83, 130n67

Agamemnon, 90

Ahaiyute, characters in Indian tales, 19, 51, 71

Ajax: his name given and career foretold, 34, 52, 85, 86; suicide of, 38, 39, 49, 100, 121n131, 121n132, 121n143

Alcestis, 44

Alcmene, 91

Alcyoneus, 17, 106, 112n21, 112n23

Alpheus, 64, 126n29

Amazons: attacked by Heracles, Peleus, Bellerophon, 12, 16, 18, 119n113

Amphiaraus: his fate in war against Thebes, 24, 76, 130n67; oracle of, 80, 87, 132n78, 133n98, 133n100

Amphion, 102, 125n28, 127n40

Amphitryon, 68, 79

Amymone, 100

Anansi, spider trickster in African tales, 55, 117n91, 122n147

Andromeda, 93, 94, 119n121

Angelia, 74, 129n59

Antaeus: slain by Heracles, 17, 54, 105, 112n21, 112n23, 117n80, 122n147; sets contest for daughter's hand, 44

Antiope, 125n28

Aphareus, 98

Aphrodite: gives magic iynx to Jason, 33, 80, 81, 117n77, 127n45; mentioned, 20, 68, 81, 131n76

Apollo: fights with Heracles, 20; fights with Python, 61; punishes Coronis and rescues unborn child, 68, 134n111; temple of, at Delphi, 71, 130n67; his love for Cyrene, 75, 108; father of Iamus and Tenerus, 85, 86, 127 n40; in Pindar, 85, 127n46; mentioned, 19, 53, 83, 88, 114n55

Archemorus, 67, 127n44

Ares, 17, 20, 47, 53, 68

Arethusa, 64, 126n29

Argonauts: folktale characteristics of, 19, 30, 32, 35, 67, 93, 94, 107; helped by Hera, 68; mentioned, 53, 60, 85, 87, 105

Ariadne, 46

Arion, 26, 101, 115n65

Aristaeus, 68, 75, 86, 130n64

Artemis: greets Heracles in land of Hyperboreans, 68; helps Taygete, 91; in Pindar, 127n45; slays Coronis and Otus, 128n54, 134n111

Asclepius: breaks tabu by using gift of healing, 69, 71, 128n52, 134n111; instructed by Chiron, 97, 135n126

Asteria, 91, 134n107

Atalanta, 44, 55

Athena: birth of, 7, 57, 58, 59, 67, 123n9; helps Perseus, 23, 31, 33, 94, 117n77; gives bridle to Bellerophon, 27, 33, 67, 117n77; invents flute music, 32, 67; gives immortality to Diomede, 48, 90, 105; mentioned, 68, 87

Atlas: holding sky, 61, 62, 119n113, 124n16, 124n23

Augeas: his stables cleaned and his

165

169